THE USBORNE BOOK OF GREEK AND NORSE LEGENDS

Cheryl Evans and Anne Millard
Illustrations by Rodney Matthews

Contents

GREEK
Myths and Legends

CONTENTS

Designed by Kim Blundell
Additional illustrations by Nick Harris, Joe McEwan,
Chris Lyon, Mark Duffin and Jan Nesbitt.
Consultant checker: Penny McCarthy

BEFORE YOU START

Before you start reading the Greek myths and legends, you may find the information below useful to find out what you can expect in the first part of this book. There are also notes on what myths and legends are and on things you need to know to understand the Greek myths and the people who invented them.

About Greek myths and legends

The first part of this book is an introduction to the most famous gods, goddesses, heroes and monsters in Greek mythology. It does not simply set out to re-tell the stories in summary form, but provides a fascinating background to Greek history, the myths as religion and, above all, detailed character information in the Who's Who (see right).

The map on page 4 allows you to follow the adventures and marks most of the places mentioned in the myths.

The main gods and goddesses are introduced on pages 12-21. Their birth, personality, best-known exploits and the places and things associated with them are all included.

There are lots of stories concerning humans whose lives were affected by the gods on pages 22-49. They range from love stories to violent battles. There is only room to tell them briefly here, but the main authors used as sources are given in the box on page 3, so you can look up their work as a start to finding out more about the myths.

Who's Who in Greek mythology

A special feature of the book is the Who's Who on pages 50-63. In it you can look up all the gods, demi-gods, heroes and monsters that appear in the book, plus others that you may come across elsewhere, though there are more that there has not been room to include.

Every name that appears in bold type (this happens the first time it occurs on a page) has a Who's Who entry. Here you can find out about its family, career, supernatural attributes and distinguishing features. It can also be used to inspire fantasy-gamers.

What is a myth?

It is difficult to define exactly what a myth is. It is generally described as a story which is the product of the imagination. However, myths were obviously more than just folk tales to the Ancient Greeks (see Religion, page 5).

Some of them seem to be attempts to explain things that would nowadays be described scientifically, such as how the world began. Ancient people had no scientific knowledge so used their imaginations to fill the gap.

Others seem to be elaborations of historical events in which human kings or heroes became like gods and did things no person could really do. This type of story is often called a legend.

Others do not fit in either of these categories and at this distance of time it is impossible to know why such gods and myths were invented and worshipped.

Combining gods

The myths evolved over many centuries. During this time, there were wars and invasions in the area that was Ancient Greece (see map on page 4).

Conquerors and settlers brought their own gods with them, which sometimes took over from, or merged with a similar deity that already existed in Greece. This gave rise to different versions of the stories about the gods and conflicting reports of their parents or birth-place.

In this book, the best-known versions have been used, which does not mean they are more correct than another.

Strange behaviour

The gods did many strange things in the myths, which the Greeks accepted in supernatural beings, although ordinary people would not have been allowed to do them. For instance, gods often married very close members of their family, such as a sister or mother. They also tended to grow up instantly and were able to do miraculous things straight away.

Some of the things humans do seem odd, too. Exposing unwanted babies to die features in many myths, for example, and was not a crime to the Ancient Greeks.

Costume note

Throughout the book, characters are shown in costumes from Classical Greece (see page 7). This style is familiar as many works of art illustrating the myths survive from this period. It does not mean that earlier people imagined the gods like this – they probably saw them in clothes from their own period.

Greek authors

Homer (about 750-700BC) The Iliad, The Odyssey.
Hesiod (about 700BC) Theogony
Bacchylides (fifth century BC) Poems.
Pindar (518-438BC) Poems
Aeschylus (525-426BC) Plays, including the Oresteia trilogy, Prometheus Bound.
Sophocles (497-405BC) Plays including Antigone, King Oedipus, Electra, Ajax.
Euripides (485-406BC) Plays, including The Bacchae, Medea, Hippolytus.

How to pronounce Greek words

Many Greek names are long and look very hard to pronounce. A pronunciation guide to each name is given in the Who's Who entries at the back of the book, but here are some general rules for pronouncing Greek words which should help you as you read through:

ae is "ee" as in Daedalus (deed-a-luss)

c is "s" when followed by an e, i or y as in Circe (sir-see), Cerberus (sir-burr-us) or Cyrene (sire-ee-nee)

c is "k" when followed by an a, u or o as in Callisto (kal-ist-toe), Curetes (kyoor-ee-teez) or Coronis (kor-on-iss)

ch is "k" as in Charon (ka-ron)

e at the end of a name is pronounced ee as in Aphrodite (aff-ro-die-tee)

es at the end of a name is "eez" as in Heracles (hair-a-kleez)

eu is "yoo", as in Zeus (zyooss)

oe is "ee" as in Oedipus (ee-dip-puss)

ph is "f" as in Hephaestos (heff-eest-oss)

MAP OF ANCIENT GREECE

THRACE

MACEDONIA

Mount Olympus

Hellespont

Troy
Mount Ida ▲

Aegean Sea

Iolcus

THESSALY

LESBOS

Mount Parnassus

SCYROS

Delphi

▲

EUBOEA

BOEOTIA

Aulis

ITHACA

Thebes ●

Athens

●

ACHAEA
Stymphalos ●

Corinth

Mt. Erymanthos

▲

Nemea ●

Marathon

ARCADIA

Mycenae

ATTICA

Olympia ●

Icarian Sea

ICARIA

Cape
Sounion

DELOS

Argos ●

SERIPHOS

● Lerna

Sparta

NAXOS

CYTHERA

Knossos

CRETE

This map shows the lands that
we now call Greece and Turkey.

What is on the map

At the time when the myths were written
down, the area was not united into these
countries, but consisted of many small states.
The most important of these are shown in
capital letters on the map, as well as the major
towns and physical features, such as

4 mountains, that appear in the myths.

You may find it helpful to refer to this map
when you are reading the stories in this book.

RELIGION

The stories told in the Greek myths formed part of the religion of Ancient Greece. They illustrated the nature of the gods and taught what pleased or angered them, but did not set out religious rules or ideals like the Bible or the Koran.

What the gods were like

This pottery drawing shows the King and Queen of the gods in their home on Mount Olympus.

The Greeks thought of their gods as being rather like themselves. They were human-shaped; got married and had children; made friends and enemies and even had human failings, like jealousy and bad-temper, which made them behave badly sometimes.

Religion and everyday life

Religion was a part of everyday life to the Greeks. They often said a quick prayer before doing something, hoping it would bring them success. Each god was responsible for some aspect of life and people worshipped the ones they found relevant. **Pan** was the god of shepherds, for example.

Temples

These are remains of the temple of Poseidon, the god of the Ocean, at Cape Sounion.

Many magnificent temples were built to the gods. Some of them have survived and you can visit them today. Priests or priestesses looked after the temples and carried out religious ceremonies. People also had shrines in their homes, where daily prayers and private ceremonies were carried out by members of the family.

This is the Temple of Apollo at Delphi.

Oracles

The Greeks believed the gods spoke to ordinary people through priests or priestesses. These messages were called **Oracles**. The most famous Oracles were spoken at Delphi (see map on page 4). It was here that **Apollo**, the sun god, killed the **Python**, a giant serpent (see page 16). A huge temple was built in his honour. The priestess, or **Pythoness**, would go into a trance then people asked her advice, believing they would hear the opinion of Apollo through her.

Festivals and drama

The Greeks had special feast days for the gods when there were processions and sacrifices. Plays were performed telling the gods' lives. Much of what we now know about Greek myths comes from these plays by **Euripides, Aeschylus, Sophocles** and others, who were writing in Classical times.

This is a Greek comic actor.

Mystery cults

This pottery picture shows a secret ceremony to Dionysus, the god of wine.

These were groups who worshipped a particular deity in secret ceremonies. Members had to pass tests before they were accepted. The cults kept their secrets so well that nobody today knows exactly what they believed.

GREEK MYTHS AND HISTORY

Greek history can be traced back over 40,000 years. No-one knows when the myths were first invented. Many come from a time before writing and were passed on by word of mouth. It is probably the spoken tradition that helped them survive upheavals when writing was destroyed or forgotten.

The changing myths

Conquerors and peaceful settlers brought their own beliefs into Greece where they were adopted or combined with the myths and gods that already existed, so they changed and developed over the centuries. They probably changed less once they were written down, but different versions of many myths survive.

Below, you can read about the main periods in Ancient Greek history and what we know about the myths at the time.

Before 6000 BC: Hunter-gatherers

The area now known as Greece was inhabited at this time by wandering tribes, hunting and living off what grew on the land. We do not know what gods they believed in.

This figure is from between 6000 and 5000 BC.

6000-2200 BC: Farmers

When farming skills were developed, people started to settle in small communities and learnt how to make pots, weave and work metal.

Clues to the religious beliefs of this early civilization are found in objects such as this marble figure, found at Sparta (see map on page 4), dating from this era. It is probably a fertility figure, as the richness of the earth for growing crops must have been very important to these farmers.

2200-1400 BC: The Minoans

This Cretan wall-painting shows bull-leaping.

Greek society advanced and developed until about 2200 BC when invaders from the north disrupted the process.

The island of Crete escaped invasion and a sophisticated civilization grew up, called Minoan after one of its kings, **Minos**. Many works of art survive, illustrating some aspects of religious life. Bulls often feature in Cretan myths and some of these were later adopted by the mainlanders into Mycenaean mythology (see below).

1600-1200 BC: The Mycenaeans

This is the Lion Gate in the great city of Mycenae, which was discovered and excavated by Heinrich Schliemann last century (see page 40).

Gradually, the mainland recovered and started to develop again. It borrowed many ideas from the Minoans, and finally became more powerful than Crete. This civilization is called Mycenaean, after its major city, Mycenae. The historical events that inspired legends about human heroes like **Jason** (see pages 32-33) took place during this period. The truth was exaggerated and embroidered to form the legends, but there is archaeological evidence for some of the events (see pages 34 and 40).

1200-700 BC: The Dark Ages

Between 1200 and 1050 BC the Mycenaean culture collapsed due to civil wars and more invasions from the north. The myths survived, passed on orally through the generations.

The poet **Homer** lived at the end of the Dark Ages. He is said to have composed two great works about the ancient legends, called the Iliad and the Odyssey. They were not written down until much later, but the stories were already 500 years old when Homer was alive.

Homer probably spoke his poems while playing the lyre. Greek schoolboys in later periods had to learn parts of his poetry by heart and every scholar could quote him.

This picture shows a poet performing his work.

700-500 BC: The Archaic Period

Between 700 and 500 BC Greece once again became rich in art, literature, science and commerce. Trade was established with many Mediterranean countries, a new form of writing was invented and coins were introduced for money. They experimented with government and social organizations but

their religion was still based on the ancient myths and legends, as can be seen from their art.

This Archaic silver coin shows a picture of Zeus, the king of the gods (see page 9).

500-336 BC: The Classical Period

This frieze shows a scene with characters in draped Classical dress.

This is probably the best-known period of Ancient Greek history. We know a lot about how people lived at this time and our image of the Ancient Greeks is probably most influenced by Classical art and literature. People lived in city-states, and much sea-faring and trading went on.

Many plays based on the myths were written during the Classical Period, and it is often these versions that have come down to us.

336-31 BC: The Hellenistic Period

This era is called the Hellenistic Period, after **Hellen**, a legendary ancestor of the Greeks (see page 48). The empire of Alexander the Great came within this period, and Greek culture spread across the Near and Middle East after his death in 323 BC.

The decline of Greece

In the last century before the birth of Christ, the Roman Empire expanded and became more powerful than Greece. The Romans were greatly influenced by the Greeks, though. They had their own gods but did not have such a complex mythology. Gradually they linked the Greek stories to their own gods until both mythologies were almost the same. The Roman names for gods and heroes adopted from Greece are given in the Who's Who on pages 50-63. *

This is a Roman statue of Mars (Greek Ares), the god of war.

*Find out more about Roman gods on page 64.

7

THE CREATION

The Ancient Greek religion tried to explain how the world began like this:

Chaos

Before anything existed there was a dark nothingness called Chaos Gradually the shape of **Mother Earth** emerged from the emptiness and formed the world.

Mother Earth's children

Mother Earth produced a son, **Uranus**, who was the sky. They then had children together. Rain fell from the sky onto the Earth, making plants grow and animals appeared from the rivers and seas. Next, many strangely-shaped monsters and giants were born. Among these were three who each had only one huge eye in the middle of their forehead and were called **Cyclopes**, meaning "wheel-eyed". Uranus treated them cruelly and banished them to the Underworld.* Later, some human-shaped giants, called **Titans**, were born who became the first gods and goddesses.

Finally, Mother Earth gave birth to the **Golden Race** who lived in an age without trouble or wars. Sadly, they had no children so the race died, though their spirits lingered on Earth to protect and help people.

The revolt of the Titans

Mother Earth could not forgive Uranus for his treatment of her first children and encouraged the Titans, led by **Cronos**, to rebel. He attacked and overcame Uranus with a sickle and took power.

Three drops of Uranus's blood fell on the earth and formed the **Erinyes**, or **Furies**. These were spirits of revenge, with a dog's head and bats' wings. They hounded murderers, especially those who killed a relative.

Another drop fell in the sea, creating foam from which the goddess **Aphrodite** was born.**

The birth of Zeus

Cronos married his sister, **Rhea**, and became King of the Titans. They had five children but Cronos had been warned that one of them would kill him, so he swallowed each one as it was born. To save her sixth child, Rhea tricked Cronos into swallowing a stone wrapped in baby's clothes and hid the real child among some lesser goddesses called **nymphs**, who brought him up safely. This child was **Zeus**.

8

*See pages 10-11 for more about the Underworld.

**Her story is told on pages 12-13.

Zeus's revenge

When he grew up, Zeus returned home in disguise and slipped a potion into Cronos's drink, making him choke. The children he had swallowed were coughed out, whole and safe. There were his daughters, **Hestia, Demeter** and **Hera**, and sons, **Pluto** and **Poseidon**.

A fierce battle then took place. Zeus freed the Cyclopes who made thunderbolts for him to hurl. They also made a forked trident for Poseidon and a helmet that made its wearer invisible for Pluto. Most of the Titans and giants sided with Cronos.

After a terrible struggle the younger gods, or **New Gods**, were victorious. The Titans were banished and one of them, called **Atlas**, was made to hold up the heavens as punishment.

Zeus became ruler of the sky and king of all the gods. Poseidon was made king of the Ocean and Pluto of the Underworld

WHAT THE WORLD WAS LIKE

The victorious gods divided the world amongst themselves. Here is what the Ancient Greeks believed their world was like.

Mount Olympus

Earth

River Styx

Ocean

Tartarus

Earth

Earth.was where humans lived. In mythical times many weird and dangerous creatures were supposed to live there, too. Greek heroes often had to fight these monsters, as you will read later in this book.

The gods frequently visited the Earth. They sometimes made friends with humans or came in disguise, rewarding or punishing people according to how they treated the gods.

Sometimes they even fell in love with humans and had children with them. Many of the heroes of the Greek myths were born in this way and were half-human and half-god.

The Underworld

Zeus's brother, **Pluto**, ruled the Underworld, or Hades. Everyone went there when they died. There were three parts:

Most ordinary people wandered around the Asphodel Fields as "shades", which were shadowy versions of their earthly selves.

Tartarus was the place of punishment for really evil people. You can read about some of the tortures they suffered on pages 26-27.

Exceptionally good or heroic people were reserved a place in the Elysian Fields. This was a golden, blissful place of rest.

You could be sent back to Earth to live another life, but if you earned a place in the Elysian Fields three times you were allowed to go the the Isles of the Blessed, and never had to leave.

The Asphodel Fields. They were grey, shadowy and misty.

Olympus

The home of the gods was the peak of Mount Olympus. There was a real mountain in the north of Greece called Mount Olympus. It probably seemed very high and remote to most of the Ancient Greeks and therefore a likely place for the gods to live. Gradually, Olympus was associated less with the actual mountain and became more an imaginary place high above the Earth.

The gods lived here like a family. Zeus married his sister, **Hera**, and they ruled as king and queen. No-one but the gods could visit Olympus, except by special invitation.

Ocean

The Earth was thought to be surrounded by a stretch of water, called Ocean. This was Poseidon's kingdom. He controlled the winds and waves so he was very important to sailors, who made sacrifices to appease him. He was very powerful, but still had to obey Zeus.

Poseidon's wife was **Amphitrite**. She was a **nereid**, which was a sea-nymph.

The Styx

The Styx was the name of the river you had to cross to enter the Underworld (see below). You had to pay the boatman, **Charon**, one obol (an Ancient Greek coin) to ferry you across.

The Elysian Fields. This was a beautiful, golden place.

Demeter, Persephone and Pluto

This is the story of how **Persephone** became Pluto's wife and Queen of the Underworld.

Demeter was goddess of plants and harvests. She made everything grow and ripen. Her daughter, Persephone, was her companion and helper.

Pluto admired Persephone and decided he wanted her as his wife. He asked Zeus's permission but did not receive a firm answer as Zeus knew that Demeter would never agree, but did not wish to offend his brother by a refusal. One day, Pluto found Persephone alone and, saying to himself that Zeus had not forbidden him to marry her, seized her and carried her down to Hades.

When Demeter found her daughter had gone, she neglected the plants and trees to search for her. Without her care, the harvests failed and everything withered and died.

After a long search, she discovered that Persephone was Pluto's prisoner and pleaded with Zeus to make him release her. The gods agreed that Zeus should do something as humans were in danger of starving since no crops would grow.

Zeus said Persephone should be freed, as long as she had not tasted any of the food of the dead. In her misery she had not eaten at all, but just before her release Pluto tempted her to try a few pomegranate seeds from his garden.

"Since you have eaten from Pluto's garden," said Zeus to Persephone, "you must spend part of each year in Hades with him. The rest you may spend on Earth with your mother."

So every year, when Persephone was with Pluto, Demeter would mourn, plants died and it was winter. When Persephone returned, Demeter was happy again, things began to blossom and it was spring.

APHRODITE, GODDESS OF LOVE

The goddess **Aphrodite** was born in a most unusual way. When **Uranus** was defeated by the **New Gods** (page 8), one drop of blood from his wounds fell in the Ocean and caused the water to froth and foam. From the foam, the fully-grown figure of Aphrodite appeared. This was supposed to have happened near the island of Cythera*.

The loveliest goddess

Aphrodite was carried in a giant scallop shell to the shores of Cyprus where she was met by the **Seasons** in the form of beautiful girls who gave her clothes and jewels to wear. Doves and sparrows flocked around her and became her special birds.

Aphrodite was the goddess of love. She existed purely to be beautiful and adored and had no other duties, as most of the Immortals did. She had a magic girdle which made whoever wore it irresistibly attractive to other people. Perhaps it was because of this that **Adonis** (see right) and **Paris** (see page 40) preferred Aphrodite even to other goddesses.

Aphrodite's marriage

Zeus decided that Aphrodite should marry his son, **Hephaestos**, the smith-god. He was strong but coarse and born lame. He worked in the gods' forge making weapons and jewellery.
Aphrodite could have had her pick of men or gods, so she was not pleased with Zeus's choice and had many lovers.

Aphrodite and Ares

The most famous of Aphrodite's lovers among the gods was **Ares**, the god of war. Hephaestos did not like his wife's behaviour and decided to teach her a lesson. He forged a net of bronze links and hung it above her bed. When the lovers were next together, he dropped the net over them and caught them like fish. He called the other gods to come and see how ridiculous they looked. He forgave Aphrodite, though, as she was so beautiful that he could not be angry with her for long.

Hephaestos, the smith-god.

Ares, the god of war.

*See map on page 4.

Aphrodite and Adonis

Aphrodite and **Persephone** both fell in love with a handsome human, called **Adonis**. He preferred Aphrodite and Persephone was jealous. She told Ares that Aphrodite loved an ordinary man more than himself. Ares was furious and, turning himself into a boar, he chased Adonis and gored him to death. Where his blood fell the first anemones grew.

Adonis was sent to the Underworld, where Persephone was queen. Aphrodite begged Zeus to let Adonis come back to her and he granted a compromise: he must stay in the Underworld during the winter but in the summer he could visit the earth and be with Aphrodite.

The wrath of Aphrodite

Despite being goddess of love, Aphrodite could become angry, just like any other goddess.

A man called **Glaucus** insulted her and this is how she punished him: the night before he was due to take part in a chariot race she gave his horses water from her sacred well and fed them a magic herb. When the race started next day, the horses went mad and crashed the chariot, killing Glaucus. They then ate their former master.

Pygmalion's reward

Aphrodite rewarded faithful followers like **Pygmalion**. He was a sculptor who worshipped Aphrodite, but could not find a suitable wife. He decided to create a statue of his ideal woman. It was such a success that he fell in love with it, although he knew his love was hopeless. Aphrodite felt sorry for him and brought the statue to life. Overjoyed, Pygamalion named her **Galatea** and they were happily married.

Aphrodite's children

Aphrodite had several children. One of her sons was **Eros**. No-one knows for sure who his father was. He made people fall in love by piercing them with his golden arrows. He was mischievous and often made the most unsuitable matches.

Aphrodite and Ares also had a daughter, called **Harmonia**. She brought back peace and harmony after war so that love, in the shape of Aphrodite, could return to the land.

Aphrodite's son by a human called **Anchises** became the hero **Aeneas** who was famous for his exploits in the Trojan War. You can find out what happened to him on page 44.

THE GODDESS ATHENE

Athene was the virgin goddess of wisdom and war. She oversaw the safety of the state and was the most important goddess after **Hera**.

The birth of Athene

There are many different versions of Athene's birth, but this is the most frequent one:

Zeus fell in love with **Metis**, the **Titaness** of wisdom. She was expecting his baby when Zeus heard a prophecy that any child Metis had would be greater than its father. Zeus could not permit this, so he turned Metis into a fly and swallowed her. This was how Zeus gained his great wisdom.

Later, Zeus was walking by Lake Triton in Libya when he developed a terrible headache. He ordered **Hephaestos** to crack his skull open, which the smith-god did, as he knew he could not harm an Immortal. From the split appeared a female figure in full armour. Zeus introduced her as his daughter, Athene.

Goddess of wisdom and war

Athene inherited Metis's wisdom and preferred to settle disputes by reasoning. If forced to fight, though, she was invincible as goddess of war. She took care of Zeus's shield (the aegis) and other battle-gear.

The owl was her special bird and she was patroness of the olive crop and of the capital city of Greece (see story oppposite).

Pallas and Athene

When she was young, Athene had a great friend, **Pallas**. One day they were practising with their spears when Athene killed her friend by accident. To show her sorrow, she put her friend's name before her own and was afterwards often known as Pallas Athene.

The invention of the flute

Athene is said to have invented the flute. She first played it at a banquet of the gods and everyone seemed to like it, except **Hera** and **Aphrodite** who would not stop giggling. (There was always rivalry between these three goddesses – see page 41.)

Athene was puzzled until she glimpsed her reflection in a pool. She soon saw what they found funny, as to play the flute she had to puff her cheeks out, which looked silly. She cursed the flute and threw it away. It was later found by **Marsyas** (see page 17).

The naming of Athens

Athene and **Poseidon** quarrelled over the naming of the greatest town in Greece. At last they agreed that whoever gave the town the best gift should also name it.

Posiedon dug his trident into the rock on which the town stood and out gushed a stream, giving access to the sea so it could become rich and powerful through trade.

Athene created the olive tree as her gift. It provided food and oil for the inhabitants and made them rich through exports, so it was judged the better gift and the town was named Athens after her. A special shrine was built to Athene on the Acropolis (the hill above Athens). It was called the Parthenon, from the word *parthenos*, meaning "maiden", which was another of Athene's titles.

The weaving contest

Athene was also goddess of crafts. This story shows how proud she was of her weaving.

Princess **Arachne** was a skilled weaver. She even boasted that she was better than Athene so the goddess challenged her to a contest. They both wove the most beautiful work they could. When they had finished, Athene was infuriated to find that Arachne's really was equal to hers, and in a jealous rage she tore the girl's weaving up. Arachne was so frightened that she tried to hang herself. Athene was then ashamed and saved Arachne from death by turning her into a spider. Ever since then spiders have woven beautiful webs.

Athene's anger

Athene's short temper features in many of the myths about her. For instance, when a man called **Tiresias** accidentally came across Athene in her bath, she blinded him for daring to look at her. She made up for her hasty action by giving him the gift of seeing the future and he advised **Oedipus** (page 29) and **Odysseus** (pages 46-47).

Another time, a crow brought Athene some bad news. Until then crows had been white but in her fury, Athene turned the unlucky messenger black and they have been black ever since.

Medusa, daughter of the sea-god **Phorcys**, suffered too. She offended Athene, who turned her into a hideous monster. The story of Medusa and her sisters (the **Gorgons**) is told on page 24.

APOLLO AND ARTEMIS

Apollo and **Artemis** were twin children of **Zeus** and the **Titaness, Leto**. Artemis was goddess of the moon and hunting and protected wild animals. Apollo was the sun god and patron of the Arts. The raven was his special bird. Both Apollo and Artemis were associated with woodland.

The birth of Artemis and Apollo

Zeus tried to keep his affair with Leto a secret, but **Hera** was not fooled. She sent her giant snake, **Python**, after poor Leto, who ran until she collapsed. The **South Wind** then lifted her over to the island of Ortygia. Here, Artemis was born. She grew up instantly and helped Leto across to the island of Delos where she gave birth to Apollo.

Chariots of the gods

The Greeks believed the sun and moon were drawn across the sky in chariots. The sun was drawn by Apollo's golden horses and the moon by Artemis's silver stags.

The punishment of Niobe

Queen **Niobe** of Thebes boasted she was better than Leto as she had seven daughters and seven sons while Leto only had one of each. To punish her, Apollo and Artemis killed all except two of her children. Niobe mourned so bitterly that Zeus took pity on her and turned her to stone on Mount Sipylus so she could no longer feel her grief, but each year when melting snow ran off the mountain, the Greeks said it was Niobe's tears.

The Muses

Apollo tamed the nine **Muses**, wild goddesses who inspired artists, and became god of the Arts. He loved music and played the lyre.

Apollo's laurel wreath

Apollo pursued a **nymph** called **Daphne**, who did not want his attentions. She ran away, praying to **Mother Earth** to save her. Just as Apollo caught her, her prayers were answered and she was turned into a laurel tree. Apollo wore a wreath of laurel leaves in her memory.

The Oracle of Apollo

Apollo hunted down the Python that had chased his mother. He killed it at Delphi and a huge temple was built to him there. He gave his priestesses the gift of telling the future. Their prophecies, or **Oracles**, were famous throughout Greece.

The quarrel over Asclepius

Apollo's arrows brought plague and death but he also had healing powers, which he passed on to his son, **Asclepius**. He became a great doctor but went too far when he began to revive the dead. **Pluto** demanded he should be stopped, as the dead were his subjects. Zeus struck Asclepius down and Apollo killed the **Cyclopes**, in revenge. Zeus would have sent Apollo to Tartarus, but for Leto's pleading.

The music contest

The **satyr, Marsyas** (you can find out about satyrs on page 18), claimed to be a better musician than Apollo, so the god suggested a competition. Marsyas played a flute he had found, not knowing it was the one Athene had cursed (page 15). They played equally well until Apollo challenged Marsyas to play his instrument upside-down and sing at the same time. This was possible with a lyre but not with a flute, so Marsyas lost. The price of losing was death and Apollo killed Marsyas.

The death of Actaeon

Actaeon was a man caught spying on Artemis while she was bathing. She turned him into a stag and her hounds hunted and killed him.

Callisto, the nymph

Artemis and her nymphs loved hunting and swore to have nothing to do with men. **Callisto** broke her vow by falling in love with Zeus. In revenge, Hera turned her into a bear and Artemis set her hounds on the nymph. Zeus saved her before she was torn apart and placed her image in the stars as the Great Bear.

Artemis and Agamemnon

Artemis was angry with King **Agamemnon**. He was preparing to send an army against Troy. She sent contrary winds so he could not set sail and demanded the sacrifice of his daughter, **Iphigenia**, to appease her. Agamemnon was about to obey, when Artemis snatched the girl and put a deer in her place. Iphigenia was taken to safety and became a priestess of Artemis.

Selene and Endymion

The Titaness Selene drove the moon's chariot. She is often confused with Artemis. A man called Endymion loved her and wished he need do nothing but think about her. Zeus granted his wish and put him in an eternal sleep in which he dreamt of Selene and never grew old.

DIONYSUS AND HERMES

Zeus was an indulgent father, even when his children misbehaved. **Hermes** and **Dionysus** were both sons of his whose behaviour was not always god-like.

Dionysus

Dionysus's mother was a princess called **Semele**, daughter of King **Cadmus** of Thebes. Zeus visited her in disguise and her family did not believe her lover was a god. They persuaded Semele to ask Zeus to prove his identity by appearing as his real self. Zeus was reluctant, but eventually gave in. He appeared as a blazing figure, with thunder and lightening crackling around him. Semele was killed instantly, as no human can look at the glory of a god and survive.

Zeus was able to save the baby Semele was expecting, however, and this was Dionysus.

Hera heard about Zeus's new son and ordered the **Titans** to tear the baby apart. They obeyed, but the **Titaness Rhea** (Zeus's mother and Dionysus's grandmother) put him back together again and brought him back to life.

Silenus and the satyrs

Dionysus grew up curly-haired and red-lipped with mischievous, sparkling eyes. He was placed in the care of **Silenus**, who was one of the many lesser deities who lived on Earth and served the Olympian gods. He had a reputation as fun-loving and irresponsible and Dionysus grew up rather wild.

Silenus and his charge travelled the world, making merry. They were often accompanied by several strange creatures called **satyrs**. These looked like young men, but had horses' ears and tails. The satyrs knew the secret of making wine from grapes and Dionysus taught this skill to people wherever he went.

Dionysus and his band were not always welcome. Silenus was often drunk and the satyrs chased nymphs and girls when the wine made them amorous.

The cult of Dionysus

Dionysus was associated with nature and the woods. His symbol was the thyrsos, a stick entwined with ivy leaves, which he usually carried.

There was a mystery cult dedicated to worshipping Dionysus. They had initiation rites and secret ceremonies which only members of the sect could attend.

Many of his followers were women. They were called **Maenads**. They danced and drank in processions through the countryside and were notorious for wild behaviour. They danced themselves into a frenzy and sometimes chased and killed animals bare-handed.

Pentheus and the Maenads

Pentheus was King of Thebes. His mother, **Agave**, was a Maenad. The king disapproved, and when Dionysus came to Thebes, Pentheus threw him in prison. Dionysus pretended to submit, but he persuaded Pentheus to spy on the Maenads to see for himself how they behaved.

Pentheus followed the women's procession and watched them from a distance. At the height of their frenzy they spotted the intruder, grabbed him and tore him limb from limb. His own mother ripped off his head, not knowing what she was doing in her trance. This was Dionysus's revenge.

Hermes

Hermes was the son of Zeus and the Titaness **Maia**. He soon got a reputation for mischief. When he was only a few days old, he stole some cattle belonging to **Apollo**. He covered their hooves with bark so they would leave no tracks and hid them away.

The lyre

Hermes used a tortoise shell and the gut from one of Apollo's cows to make the instrument called a lyre.

Hermes is caught

Silenus and the satyrs helped Apollo search for his stolen cattle. They were drawn to the music that Hermes was playing on his lyre. When they saw the instrument and the cow-gut used for its strings, they knew they had found the thief. Apollo was furious and would not listen to any excuses. Eventually, Hermes stopped trying to appease him and simply played the lyre in the hope of calming him down. Apollo, as god of music, was charmed by the instrument and agreed to take the lyre in payment for his stolen cows. That is how Apollo came to own the lyre for which he became so famous.

Messenger of the gods

Zeus was amused by the exploits of Hermes, but could not allow them to continue. He decided Hermes must have a task to keep him out of trouble and made him the messenger of the gods and patron of travellers. Zeus gave him a winged helmet and sandals so he could travel faster.

Since he had bargained so well with Apollo, he became god of trade and treaties; and because of the incident with Apollo's cattle, thieves and liars prayed to him, hoping for sympathy.

Hermes is supposed to have helped invent the alphabet, boxing and gymnastics, too.

PROMETHEUS AND MANKIND

The **Titan, Prometheus**, was wise and thoughtful. His name means "forethought" which suited him well. He took the side of **Zeus** in the war against **Cronos** (page 8), and so was not banished like the other Titans when the **New Gods** came to power.

Making the first people

Prometheus is supposed to have created the human race. This is how it came about:

The first people on Earth were the **Golden Race** (see page 8). They disappeared as they had no children and Zeus replaced them with the **Silver Race**. Unfortunately, they started to do all sorts of evil things so Zeus imprisoned them in Tartarus.

Zeus was discouraged by this failure, and asked Prometheus to try his hand at making a race to live on Earth. The Titan had the idea of making mortals that looked like the gods so that gods and humans could understand each other better. This was the **Bronze Race**.

The trick

Prometheus was fond of the people he had created and helped them whenever he could.

There was a quarrel about which part of a sacrifice should be dedicated to Zeus. Prometheus found a way of settling it in mankind's favour. He divided a sacrificed bull into two bags. In one he put the bones with a few bits of nice meat on top. In the other he put the rest of the meat, covered with the unappetizing stomach. He invited Zeus to choose which bag he would like as his portion. Naturally, Zeus chose the one that looked nicest, although it was full of bones. From that time, the bones were always Zeus's share of a sacrifice, leaving most of the meat for the people to eat.

Zeus was furious when he discovered the trick, though he could not alter his choice. As punishment, he refused to let humans have fire, the gift he had intended for them, so they shivered in the dark and ate raw meat.

The gift of fire

Prometheus felt very sorry for mankind, and with the aid of **Athene**, his faithful pupil and friend, he stole some fire from Zeus's palace and showed people how to use it. They could then cook, make metal tools to cultivate the land and keep warm and this was how civilization began.

When Zeus found out what Prometheus had done, it was too late to take the fire away again but he punished Prometheus horribly.

Prometheus's punishment

Zeus had Prometheus bound to a rock with unbreakable chains and ordered an eagle to rip out his liver. Despite the pain, Prometheus could not die, as he was immortal. His liver was renewed every night and the torture started again every morning.

Many centuries later, Zeus allowed Prometheus to be rescued by **Heracles** (see page 39).

The flood

Zeus became more and more displeased with mankind. Once, when he visited Earth in disguise, a family tried to feed him human flesh. Zeus decided people had become so wicked that they did not deserve to live and sent a great flood to drown them.

Prometheus dared to interfere again and warned one Earthly king of the coming flood. This was his son, **Deucalion**.

Deucalion and his wife, **Pyrrha**, built a boat and survived the flood, which lasted nine days and nights. When the water subsided, the boat landed safely on Mount Parnassus (see map, page 4). Husband and wife climbed onto the land and sacrificed to Zeus in thanks.

Zeus had begun to regret destroying the whole human race, and was glad when he found these two had survived. He sent the **Titaness, Themis**, to help them. She told them to walk along, throwing stones over their shoulders without looking back. They did what she said, and all the stones thrown by Deucalion turned into men and those thrown by Pyrrha into women so the human race started again. These were the people of the Age of Heroes, which ended with the Trojan War (see pages 40-43).

Pandora

Zeus punished mankind, too, for accepting Prometheus's gift. He asked Hephaestos to shape a woman in his forge. The King of the gods then breathed life into her and sent her to Prometheus's brother, **Epimetheus**. He gave her a jar, which he strictly forbade her to open, to take with her.*

Prometheus had warned his brother never to accept anything from Zeus, but Epimetheus welcomed the visitor and finally married her.

She was called **Pandora** and was very lovely, but very inquisitive. She longed to know what was in Zeus's jar and one day she could not resist peeping inside.

Out of it flew all the evils that plague the world—sickness, age, sin and death. As Pandora stared in horror at the empty jar, one last thing emerged. It was Hope, and it meant that people should never despair.

*Pandora is often said to have had a box, but "jar" is a better translation of the Greek word.

ZEUS'S LOVERS

Although **Zeus** was married to **Hera**, he often fell in love with other beautiful women. Many of the children from these affairs became heroes or rulers. Hera sometimes tried to punish the women or their children, but Zeus protected them from the worst of her anger. Here are some of their stories.

Io

When Zeus fell in love with **Io**, he turned her into a white cow to hide her from his wife. Hera found out and tethered Io, leaving her hundred-eyed servant, **Argus**, on guard.

Zeus sent **Hermes** to soothe Argus to sleep by playing his lyre. One by one, Argus closed all his eyes. Hermes swiftly struck off his head and freed Io.

Hera was furious and sent a gadfly to sting her rival. The insect chased Io all the way to Egypt. Here, she became a woman again and a priestess of the Egyptian goddess, Isis.

Europa

Princess **Europa** of Tyre was on the beach when Zeus appeared, disguised as a white bull. She was afraid at first but the bull was so handsome and gentle that she soon started to play and garlanded him with flowers. She even got on his back to go for a ride.

At that moment, the bull plunged into the sea and carried her off to Crete, where she lived and had three sons with Zeus.

Later, Europa married the King of Crete who made her eldest son, **Minos**, his heir.*

Danae

King **Acrisius** was warned by an **Oracle** that he would be killed by his grandson. He locked his daughter, **Danae**, in a tower so she could never marry and have children.

He could not keep her from Zeus, though. He entered her prison as a shower of gold and Danae had his son, **Perseus**.**

Acrisius could not bear to kill them, despite the Oracle, so he set them adrift in a boat. Zeus guided the boat safely to the island of Seriphos.

*See page 34.

**You can read what became of Perseus on page 24.

Alcmene

Alcmene was already married when Zeus fell in love with her. She refused to betray her husband, so the god played a trick on her.

Zeus disguised himself as Alcmene's husband and went to her just when he was due back from war. She greeted Zeus fondly – and had a shock when her real husband arrived next day.

The couple guessed the truth, but could do nothing about it. Alcmene had Zeus's son and called him **Heracles**, ("Glory of Hera"), to appease Zeus's wife. This did not work, and Hera made Heracles's life extremely difficult, as you can read on pages 37-39.

Leda

Leda was Queen of Sparta, married to King **Tyndareus**. One day, she was bathing in a stream when a handsome swan swam up.

The swan was Zeus in disguise. He became Leda's lover and she produced a beautiful blue egg, from which were hatched four children, two belonging to Zeus and two to her husband.

Zeus's children were **Helen**, the most beautiful woman on Earth, for whom the Trojan War was fought (see pages 40-43), and the hero **Polydeuces**. The children of Tyndareus were **Clytemnestra** and **Castor**.

Thetis

Thetis was a **nereid**, a sea-goddess who could change shape at will. It was predicted that her son would be greater than its father. Zeus was in love with her but could not risk having such a son. He decided she must marry a mortal, **Peleus**, although he knew she would resist.

Peleus found Thetis on the seashore and seized her. She changed shape from woman to fire, water, lion, serpent and cuttlefish, but Peleus held on. His courage impressed Thetis and she agreed to marry him.

All the gods were invited to their wedding, except **Eris**, the goddess of spite. She got her revenge as you can see on page 41.

PERSEUS

Perseus and his mother, **Danae**, landed on the island of Seriphos and were looked after by King **Polydictes**.

Polydictes's challenge

Later, Polydictes tried to persuade Danae to marry him. She refused. He felt she might change her mind if her son went away, so he teased Perseus for preferring his mother's company to doing brave deeds like other young men. He said Perseus should prove his courage, by killing **Medusa** the **Gorgon**.

Perseus hunts Medusa

Medusa had been turned into a hideous monster by **Athene** (see page 15). She had snakes instead of hair and anyone who looked at her was turned to stone. She and her two sisters, also monsters, were called Gorgons.

As Athene had created Medusa, she decided to help Perseus kill her. She gave him a shining shield and told him to look only at Medusa's reflection, never directly at her. **Hermes** gave him a sickle and sent him to the **nymphs** in the Underworld to borrow **Pluto's** helmet of invisibility (see page 9). They also gave him a magic wallet and winged sandals.

Perseus sought Medusa out and attacked her with his magic weapons. He watched her in the polished shield, and managed to cut off her head, which he put in the magic wallet. He escaped on his winged sandals.

The freeing of Andromeda

Flying home, Perseus saw a beautiful princess chained to a rock and fell in love. This was **Andromeda**. Her parents had boasted she was lovelier than the **nereids** so **Poseidon** had flooded their land. To appease him, Andromeda was to be sacrificed to a sea-monster.

Perseus waited for the monster and killed it. He then freed Andromeda and married her.

When they returned to Seriphos, Polydictes was about to force Danae into marriage. Outraged, Perseus held up Medusa's head, the king looked at it and was turned to stone.

The Oracle is right again

One day, Perseus took part in some important Games. As he threw a discus it was caught by the wind and accidentally killed an old man. This proved to be **Acrisius**, his own grandfather, whom he had not seen since birth. The tragedy had been foretold by an **Oracle** (see page 5) and was unavoidable.

WICKED WOMEN

Wickedness, greed, pride and stupidity were all punished by the gods in appropriate ways. Amongst the characters whose behaviour offended the gods were several wicked women. The misdeeds of some of the most famous ones are told below.

Phaedra

Phaedra was the second wife of the hero, **Theseus** (see pages 34-36). She was jealous of **Hippolytus**, Theseus's son by his first wife. She made up a story that Hippolytus had attacked her. Theseus was appalled and asked **Poseidon** to punish his son.

As Hippolytus drove his chariot along the beach, Poseidon sent a huge wave which scared his horses, making them bolt. There was a terrific crash and Hippolytus was killed.

When Theseus learnt that Phaedra had lied, she hanged herself to escape his anger.

Danaus's daughters

Danaus and **Aegyptus** were grandsons of Poseidon. One had 50 sons and the other, 50 daughters. When their father died, the twins quarrelled over their inheritance. Aegyptus suggested that his sons should marry Danaus's daughters to make peace.

An **Oracle** warned Danaus and his daughters that Aegyptus planned to kill them, so they ran away. Aegyptus chased them, trapped them in the city of Argos and starved them into defeat.

So the marriages took place, but Danaus gave each daughter a huge, sharp hair-pin and told them to kill their husbands. All except one of them used the pins.

The murderesses survived, but when they died they went to Tartarus (page 10) where they were made to carry water from one place to another in leaking jars so they could never complete the task.

Ino

King **Athamas** had two children, **Phrixus** and **Helle**. Their mother was **Nephele** the cloud-woman (see page 26).

The king abandoned Nephele to marry **Ino**. Ino hated his children and plotted against them.

Ino lit a fire under the grain store, which dried the seed up so it would not grow. The crops failed and the people starved.

Athamas sent to the Oracle at Delphi to ask what to do. Ino bribed the messenger to say the Oracle's advice was to sacrifice his son.

Athamas sadly prepared to kill Phrixus, but **Hera** sent a golden ram to rescue him and Helle. She also made Athamas so angry that he forced Ino to jump off a cliff and drown.

The ram flew east, but as it crossed from Europe to Asia, Helle fell from its back and drowned. The sea was called the Hellespont (sea of Helle) after her. Phrixus landed in Colchis and sacrificed the ram to **Zeus** in thanks. Its fleece became the object of a great quest (see pages 32-33).

Scylla

The city of Megara and its king, **Nisus**, were under attack by King **Minos** of Crete. Nisus's daughter, **Scylla**, watched Minos from the city walls and fell in love with him.

Nisus had a magic lock of hair. As long as it was in his possession, his city was safe. Scylla stole the hair, slipped out of the city and gave it to Minos.

Minos won the battle and killed Nisus, but was so disgusted by Scylla's betrayal that he sailed without her. She swam after him, but her father's ghost swooped down on her as an eagle and she drowned.

EVIL MEN

The stories on this page are about men who angered the gods and were duly punished. It was not only humans that had to be taught a lesson, however.

Sometimes, Zeus had to punish gods for disobeying him or abusing their power.

Daedalus and Icarus

Daedalus was an inventor. He designed the maze for the **Minotaur** on Crete (see page 34). He offended King **Minos** who imprisoned him and his son, **Icarus**.

Daedalus planned an ingenious escape by making wings for them both out of feathers, wax and thread. The wings worked and they flew from the window of their prison.

Icarus was thrilled at flying like a bird. Despite his father's warnings not to get carried away, he flew higher and higher until he was so close to the sun that the wax melted and the wings broke apart. He fell into the sea and drowned near the island now called Icaria after him.

Ixion

Ixion was a murderer. He had killed his future father-in-law. Generously, **Zeus** was prepared to forgive him, but instead of being grateful, Ixion planned to carry off Zeus's wife, **Hera**.

Zeus could not believe he would really be that wicked, so he made a double of his wife out of clouds to see what would happen. To his dismay, Ixion pounced and carried the

cloud-woman, **Nephele**, away, proving how evil he was.

As punishment, Zeus ordered **Hermes** to tie Ixion to a wheel of fire, which he set rolling endlessly round the sky.

Phaethon

Phaethon was the son of the **Titan, Helios. Apollo** was god of the sun, but Helios was responsible for driving it across the sky in his chariot. Phaethon longed to have a go at the reins. He begged so hard that at last his father agreed to let him try.

At first Phaethon drove well, but then he began to show off. He rode so high that the Earth froze, then came so low that it scorched. Zeus was appalled and threw a thunderbolt at Phaethon, who fell from the chariot and was killed.

Sisyphus

Sisyphus was most unpleasant. He seduced his niece, took his brother's throne and betrayed Zeus's secrets. Zeus ordered **Pluto** to take him to Hades.

Sisyphus slyly asked Pluto to try on his chains to show how they worked. Sisyphus quickly secured them and took Pluto prisoner. This caused havoc, as the dead could not enter Hades without Pluto as guide.

Ares rescued Pluto and Sisyphus was sent to Tartarus, where he was made to roll a boulder up a steep hill. When he reached the top, the stone rolled back down. He tried again and again, but each time it was the same, so he could never finish his task.

Midas

To thank King **Midas** for looking after **Silenus, Dionysus** granted him a wish. The greedy king asked that everything he touched should turn to gold. He regretted it when even his daughter became a gold statue and food turned to gold when he tried to eat. He pleaded with Dionysus to undo the wish, which he did.

Later, Midas offended **Apollo** who gave him ass's ears. He hid the shameful ears under

his cap, but his barber discovered them. The barber was sworn to secrecy, but longed to tell someone. He dug a hole, spoke the secret into it, then filled it in, hoping it was safely buried. Some reeds grew on the spot and when they rustled in the wind, they whispered what was in the earth below and everyone knew how silly Midas was.

Tantalus

Tantalus was Zeus's friend and dined with the gods. He abused this honour by stealing ambrosia and nectar, the food and drink of the gods, and giving it to his friends on Earth. He then invited the gods to a banquet and decided to test for himself whether they were really all-knowing.

He killed and served up his own son, **Pelops**, at the feast, knowing that it was forbidden to eat human flesh. The gods knew at once what was on their plates and Zeus was so angry that he banished Tantalus to Tartarus (see page 10).

He was made to stand in a pool of water with fruit hanging just out of his reach; if he tried to eat or drink, the fruit and water moved away, so he was eternally tormented by hunger and thirst.

27

FATE AND THREE HEROES

The Ancient Greeks believed in Fate, which meant they thought their lives were predetermined by the gods. Even heroes were subjects of Fate, and had to suffer if they displeased the gods.

Bellerophon

Bellerophon was the grandson of **Sisyphus***. He was wrongly accused of trying to seduce the wife of King **Proteus** of Argos. Angrily, Proteus sent Bellerophon from his court with a letter to deliver to the King of Lycia.

The letter asked the King of Lycia to kill the person who brought it but he did not want to offend the **Furies** by murdering a guest. Instead, he asked Bellerophon to kill the beast called the **Chimaera** to pay for his hospitality. The Chimaera was a fire-breathing monster with the head of a lion, the body of a goat and a serpent's tail. The king was sure Bellerophon would fail and be killed.

Athene decided to help Bellerophon. She lent him her winged horse, **Pegasus**, and he flew over the Chimaera and plunged his spear down its throat.

Bellerophon then helped the king by flying above his enemies and pelting them with rocks. The king could not believe the hero deserved to die after this and they became friends. Bellerophon even married his daughter.

After a while Bellerophon became too proud. He tried to fly to Olympus on Pegasus. No human was allowed in the home of the gods without an invitation, so Bellerophon had to be punished. **Zeus** sent a fly that drove Pegasus wild. The hero was thrown from his back and landed in a thorn bush. He was blinded and lamed, ending his life homeless and alone.

28

*See page 27.

Orion

Orion was **Poseidon's** son, a great hunter and a very handsome man.

This is the star group called Scorpio.

He offended several of the Immortals. The goddess **Eos** was in love with him, but he abandoned her to hunt with **Artemis. Apollo** was on guard in case Orion insulted or hurt his sister, knowing how he had behaved with Eos.

Orion then angered **Mother Earth** by boasting that he could kill all the wild animals and monsters in the world, which were of course all Mother Earth's children.

She sent a giant scorpion to attack Orion. He fought bravely but soon realized that it could not be killed by mortal weapons. He dived into the sea to escape, hoping to reach the island of Delos, where Eos would protect him.

It was Artemis who was waiting for him on Delos, though. Apollo joined her and bet that she could not hit the small shape bobbing out at sea with her arrow. Apollo knew very well that this was Orion but Artemis accepted his challenge, shot accurately and killed him.

When she realized what she had done, she begged **Asclepius** (see page 17) to bring Orion back to life, but he was forbidden to do so by Zeus. So Artemis put the image of Orion among the stars, where he is forever chased across the sky by the scorpion (the star sign, Scorpio).

These are the stars called Orion.

Oedipus

Your Fate was unavoidable, however unfair it seemed, as in the case of **Oedipus**, son of King **Laius** and Queen **Jocasta** of Thebes.

An **Oracle** said Oedipus would kill his father and marry his mother, so Laius exposed him on a mountain to die so it could not come true.

A shepherd found the baby and took him to Corinth where the king and queen adopted him. He believed these were his real parents and when he heard the prophecy he ran away, hoping to avoid his fate.

On the road, Oedipus quarrelled with a man he met. Neither would step out of the other's way. There was a fight and Oedipus killed him. He did not know it, but the man was Laius, so part of the prophecy had come true.

Near Thebes, Oedipus met the **Sphinx**, a beast with a woman's head, lion's body, serpent's tail and eagle's wings. She asked passers-by a riddle:

"What goes on four legs in the morning, two at midday and three in the evening, and is weakest when it has most legs?"

She killed anyone who could not answer.* No-one had ever escaped until Oedipus answered correctly. The Sphinx flung herself over a cliff in humiliation.

The Thebans were delighted and made Oedipus king, as Laius was dead. He married the dead king's wife, Jocasta, and so unknowingly fulfilled the other half of the prophecy.

All went well for a while, but then a plague struck Thebes. The Oracle said the only cure was to avenge Laius's death. Oedipus cursed the murderer, not knowing it was himself.

The seer, **Tiresias** (page 15), revealed the truth and enquiries in Corinth confirmed it.

Jocasta hanged herself in shame and Oedipus blinded himself with her brooch pin. He left Thebes with his daughter, **Antigone**, and died near Athens. Theseus buried him honourably.

*Answer in the Who's Who entry for the Sphinx, page 62.

LOVE STORIES

The Greek myths are full of love stories, both tragic and happy. Those who suffered for love were often rewarded by the gods, while the hard-hearted were taught a lesson.

Echo and Narcissus

The **nymph, Echo**, distracted **Hera** while **Zeus** chased mountain nymphs. As punishment, Hera condemned her never to make a comment of her own again. She could only repeat the last words that other people said.

Poor Echo fell in love with **Narcissus**. He was very handsome but also hard-hearted and vain. She followed him, helplessly repeating the ends of his phrases, until she faded away with sorrow, leaving only her voice.

Narcissus made many other lovers unhappy until **Artemis** decided to punish him. She showed him his own reflection in a pool and he fell in love with it. Realizing he would never love anyone else as well, he stabbed himself to death in despair. The flower called narcissus sprang up from his blood.

Oreithyia and Boreas

The serpent-tailed god of the north wind, **Boreas**, fell in love with a mortal named **Oreithyia**, an Athenian princess. She was dancing in a festival when he swooped down, carried her off and married her.

For his wife's sake Boreas always had a soft spot for Athens. Once, when the Persians were attacking by sea, he sent a storm which scattered their fleet and saved the city.

Phyllis

Phyllis and **Acamas** were devoted lovers. Acamas was the son of the hero, **Theseus**, and went off to fight in the Trojan Wars, which lasted for ten years (see pages 40-43).

Phyllis pined without him, and would have died, but Athene took pity on her and turned her into an almond tree.

When Acamas returned and heard what had happened, he kissed the trunk of the almond tree in sorrow. The tree burst into flower even though its leaves had not yet opened; ever since the almond has flowered before its leaves appear.

Orpheus and Eurydice

Orpheus was the best musician in Greece. When he returned from his travels with **Jason** (see pages 32-33) he married his beloved **Eurydice**. Soon after, she died of a snake-bite.

Orpheus went to the Underworld to beg **Pluto** to free her. He played such sweet music on his lyre that Pluto was charmed and agreed to let Eurydice go – if Orpheus could lead her from his kingdom without looking back.

Orpheus set off and Eurydice followed, but the temptation to turn round was too great. He looked too soon and lost her for good. Orpheus was so unhappy that he forgot to make sacrifices to **Dionysus** and the **Maenads** (see page 19) tore him apart. He was buried at the foot of Mount Olympus and birds were said to sing more sweetly there than anywhere else.

Orpheus joined Eurydice in Hades, and his lyre became the group of stars called Lyra.

Psyche

Psyche's parents boasted that their daughter was as lovely as **Aphrodite**. In revenge, the goddess told **Eros** to make Psyche fall in love with a monster. Psyche was taken to a remote mountain-side to await her Fate.

Eros went to obey Aphrodite, but grazed himself with his arrow and fell in love with Psyche. He took her to a beautiful palace and

visited her there, making himself invisible, as she must never discover who he was.

Psyche's sisters visited her and were so jealous that they suggested her invisible lover must be a monster as predicted and that she ought to find out. One night, she shone a light on Eros while he slept. He and the palace vanished at once. Psyche was heart-broken. **Demeter** advised her to appeal to Aphrodite, who might then let Eros return.

Aphrodite tested Psyche to see if she was worthy of Eros. She asked her to separate a huge mixed pile of wheat and barley grains. An army of ants, sent by Eros, came along and did the job for her. Aphrodite next sent her to **Persephone** with a jar, saying it contained beauty cream. Psyche could not resist opening it, but it actually contained the Sleep of Death and Psyche was overcome.

Eros managed to revive her and Zeus decided to help. He soothed Aphrodite and made Psyche immortal so she could be with Eros.

JASON AND THE GOLDEN FLEECE

Jason was heir to the throne of Iolcus, but his uncle, **Pelias**, stole the crown when Jason was a baby. The deposed king and his son were banished, but when Jason grew up he came to claim his crown. Pelias said Jason could be his heir if he fetched the golden fleece from Colchis. The fleece came from the ram that **Hera** had sent to rescue **Phrixus** (see page 25). Pelias hoped Jason would never return.

The Argonauts
Jason had a great ship built and gathered a crew of heroes to accompany him. The ship was called Argo and its crew, the **Argonauts.**

King Phineus's advice
On the way, they visited King **Phineus** for his advice on the dangers ahead. He agreed to help if they could rid him of the **Harpies**. These were birds with a woman's head that screeched and snatched food, so their victims could not eat or rest. The heroes attacked the horrible birds, who clawed and slashed, but were driven out to sea at last.

Phineus knew how to get past the **Clashing Rocks**. They formed a lethal barrier at the entrance to the Straits of Bosphorous. They crashed shut if a ship tried to pass between them and crushed it.

"Send a bird through first," Phineus said, "to make the rocks crash shut. As they reopen, row between quickly before they shut again." The heroes did as he said and got through safely, though the bird lost a few tail-feathers.

Jason's test
At Colchis, Jason told King **Aeetes** their mission. He did not intend to let Jason take the fleece. He said that to prove himself Jason must harness two fire-breathing bulls, plough a field with them and plant some dragon's teeth. He was sure Jason would be killed, but the gods made his daughter, the witch **Medea**, fall in love with Jason and help him.

Medea
Medea gave Jason a potion to protect him from the bulls' breath while he ploughed. When he planted the dragon's teeth, armed soldiers sprang up and attacked. He took Medea's advice and threw a stone among them. One soldier thought another had hit him, fighting broke out and they all killed each other.

The journey home

Aeetes chased them and was catching up, so cruel Medea killed her half-brother. She threw his limbs overboard, knowing her father would stop to pick them up and stop the chase.

Some say they crossed Europe by river, emerging in the north and sailing past Britain, France and Spain on their way home. They met more dangers, such as the **sirens** on Capri. These were sea-nymphs who sang so beautifully that they lured sailors onto the jagged rocks. Orpheus played his lyre to drown their voices and they sailed safely by.

Approaching Crete, they were attacked by King **Minos's** bronze giant, **Talos**. He hurled rocks at strangers who came too near. Their weapons could not hurt him, but the heroes distracted him while Medea removed the pin which kept his life-force in. Talos then collapsed.

Medea's evil schemes

Back in Iolcus, Medea tricked Pelias's daughters into killing him. She said they could restore his youth by boiling him in a cauldron. The throne was then free for Jason, but the people were sickened by Medea's deeds and banished them both.

Medea was heiress to the throne of Corinth so they made their way there and Jason became king. He ruled well at first, but grew arrogant and broke his oath to Medea by planning to marry a princess, **Glaucis**.

Medea sent Glaucis a magic robe and crown as gifts. When she put them on, they burst into flames and killed her. Medea fled. Some say she killed her children first, others that the Corinthians slew them in revenge.

Jason's death

Jason lost the gods' favour and ended his life an outcast. He roamed until he came across the rotting hull of the Argo. Here, he sat down and was dreaming of the past when the prow fell and killed him. His death was a warning to anyone who broke his oath.

The golden fleece

Medea then told Jason how to deal with the dragon-serpent guarding the fleece. This monster had a dragon's head and serpent's body and was never known to sleep. On Medea's advice, Jason asked **Orpheus** to play a lullaby on his lyre until finally the beast closed its eyes. Jason grabbed the fleece and ran back to the Argo, taking Medea and her half-brother with him. Jason swore to marry Medea and be faithful to her.

THESEUS

Theseus was a popular Greek hero. His best-known adventure was on Crete, where he fought the **Minotaur** (see picture, opposite).

Before you read the story you may be interested to find out a bit about the Minoan culture on Crete (see box, below).

Theseus and the Minotaur

Theseus was brought up by his mother. No-one was sure who his father was as both **Poseidon** and King **Aegeus** of Athens had loved his mother. She hoped that Aegeus would make the boy his successor.

Aegeus's wife was the witch **Medea**, who had previously been married to **Jason** (see pages 32-33). When Theseus grew up and came to court, Medea recognized him through her magic powers. She did not want the king to discover his identity, since she wanted her own son by Aegeus to be the only heir to his throne.

Medea persuaded Aegeus that Theseus was a dangerous enemy and prepared a cup of poison which she gave him. As he was about to drink it, the king recognized the sword Theseus was wearing. He had given it to Theseus's mother as a gift for their son, if they should have one.

Theseus was welcomed and declared as successor to Aegeus. Medea escaped in her serpent-drawn chariot. Her evil plans had failed again.

Minos's victims

Several years before, King Minos's son had been killed in Athens. In compensation, Minos demanded that fourteen young Athenians should be sent to Crete every nine years to be fed to the Minotaur.

The Minotaur was a dreadful beast with the head and shoulders of a bull and the body of a man. It fed on human flesh and was kept in a maze called the Labyrinth, which had been designed by the craftsman, **Daedalus** (see page 49). No-one who entered the maze ever came out alive.

THESEUS AND THE MINOTAUR CONTINUED

When the time came for the next victims to go to Crete, Theseus said he would go as one of them and try to kill the Minotaur. The king was afraid for his son. He could hardly bear waiting for news, and asked the sailors who took Theseus to Crete to hoist white sails when they returned if all was well and Theseus was alive.

Minos's dare

Minos recognized Theseus among the Athenians and taunted him about who his father was. He dared Theseus to prove he was the son of Poseidon by retrieving a ring that he threw into the sea. Theseus dived after it, praying to Poseidon for help. The **nereids** found the ring for him and **Amphitrite** presented him with the crown worn by **Thetis** on her wedding day. He emerged from the water triumphant with Minos's ring and the crown.

Into the Labyrinth

Minos's daughter, **Ariadne**, fell in love with Theseus when she saw him among the victims. She offered to help him kill the Minotaur if he would marry her and he agreed. She gave him a magic ball of twine. He tied one end to the entrance of the maze, then followed as it unwound and led him into the centre of the Labyrinth where the Minotaur lurked.

Theseus's return

There was a terrible fight, but Theseus overcame the Minotaur at last and followed the path marked by the magic twine out of the Labyrinth, leading the other young Athenians, who had been saved from their Fate.

They escaped by boat and took Ariadne with them. On their way home they stopped at the island of Naxos. Here, while Ariadne was sleeping, ungrateful Theseus sailed off without her, forgetting that he owed his success to her and had promised to marry her. When she woke up alone and realized she had been abandoned, she cried to the gods for revenge.

The god, **Dionysus**, happened to be passing Naxos soon after. He saw Ariadne and fell in love with her. She became his wife and he soon granted her revenge by making Theseus so glad to be going home that he forgot to give the order to raise white sails and approached Athens with black sails on the mast. When Aegeus saw them, he believed his son must be dead, jumped into the sea and drowned himself in despair. The sea where this happened was called Aegean after him.

What became of Theseus

In these sad circumstances, Theseus became king of Athens in his father's place. He married **Hippolyte**, an **Amazon** queen. She later died fighting at Theseus's side in battle. Their son, **Hippolytus**, was killed through the wickedness of Theseus's jealous second wife, **Phaedra** (see page 25).

After these tragic deaths, Theseus became careless of his kingly duties and went adventuring again. He kidnapped the young **Helen** of Troy (see page 41), whose brothers had to raid Athens to rescue her. He also went to Tartarus with his friend, **Pirithous**, who planned to snatch **Persephone**. They were caught by the gods and put in chains of forgetfulness. Theseus was later rescued by **Heracles** but while he was away, his throne was taken from him.

Theseus settled on the island of Scyros, and died there, but his love for Athens outlasted his death. When the city was about to lose the battle of Marathon, his ghost appeared to inspire the troops and led them to victory. After that his body was brought home and buried with honours in Athens.

Amazons

The Amazons were a mythical race of warrior women from south-west Asia. They were very fierce and were not generally sympathetic to men. They were sometimes said to cut their right breast off so they could draw their bowstring more easily.

HERACLES

One of the Greeks' favourite heroes was **Heracles**. You may know him as Hercules, which is the Roman version of his name. He was exceptionally strong and brave, but **Hera** made his life extremely difficult as he reminded her of **Zeus's** infidelity (see page 23).

The baby Heracles

When Heracles was a baby, Hera sent two deadly serpents to his cradle to kill him. Heracles strangled them both, surprising everyone with his strength.

Hera's revenge

Heracles married **Megara**, had a family and became famous for his great courage. Hera was jealous of his happiness and drove him mad so that he killed his wife and children. When he recovered and saw what he had done he was horrified and asked the **Oracle** how he could make amends. He was told to offer himself as a slave to King **Eurystheus**.

Eurystheus set Heracles twelve "impossible" tasks. If he could do them all, he would get rid of his guilt and become an Immortal. They were called his Twelve Labours and are described below and over the page.

1. To kill the Nemean lion

This lion from Nemea had a hide so tough that no weapon could pierce it. Heracles had to strangle it with his bare hands. Afterwards, he wore the lion's skin as protection.

2. To destroy the Lernaean Hydra

In the swamps of Lerna lived the Hydra. It had a dog-like body and nine serpent's heads, which grew again each time they were cut off. Heracles had to strike off each head and seal the neck with a burning torch before he could kill it.

3. To capture the Cerynean hind alive

This deer had hooves of bronze, horns of gold and was sacred to **Artemis**. Catching it alive was even more difficult than killing it. Heracles stalked it for a whole year before being able to catch it in a net and carry it to **Eurystheus**.

4. To trap the Erymanthian boar

Heracles drove the enormous, fierce creature into a deep snowdrift and when it was trapped he tied it with chains.

5. To clean the Augean stables

The stables of King **Augeus** had not been cleaned for years and were piled high with dung. Heracles was told to clean them thoroughly in one day. Not even Heracles could have done it by himself. He succeeded, though, by diverting the course of a nearby river so that it swept through the stables and washed all the muck away.

6. To get rid of the Stymphalian birds

These were man-eating birds with bronze beaks, claws and wings. Heracles startled them with a great shout so that they flew up, then shot them with his arrows.

7. To capture the Cretan bull

This bull was father of the **Minotaur** (see page 34). It ran wild on Crete, causing great damage. Heracles managed to master the animal and take it back to Eurystheus by boat.

8. To round up the mares of Diomedes

These horses fed on human flesh and were extremely wild. Their master was called **Diomedes**. Heracles killed Diomedes first and fed him to the mares. When they were full they were relatively calm and he got them under control.

9. To fetch Hippolyte's girdle, or belt

Hippolyte was Queen of the **Amazons** (see page 36). She was quite happy to give Heracles her girdle, but **Hera** made the Amazons think he was hurting her, so they attacked and he had to fight their whole army to get the belt.

10. To fetch the cattle of Geryon

Spain

Gibraltar and Ceuta were said to be the remains of the Pillars of Heracles.

Gibraltar

Ceuta

Morocco

These cattle lived on an island in the far west, guarded by **Orthrus**, a two-headed dog, and the herdsman **Geryon** who had three bodies above the waist. Heracles killed them both and drove the cattle home. On his way west, he placed two pillars, one in Spain and one in Morocco, to guard the Mediterranean.

11. To fetch the golden apples of the Hesperides

The golden apples belonged to Hera. They were kept by the **Hesperides** who were the daughters of the **Titan, Atlas.**

Heracles did not know where the Hesperides kept the apples so he went to ask their father. Atlas had to support the weight of the heavens on his shoulders (see page 9), but he said that if Heracles would just take his place for a while, he would go and fetch the apples himself. Heracles agreed and Atlas set off.

Atlas returned with the apples, but had enjoyed his freedom so much that he refused to take his burden back. He said he would take the apples to Eurystheus himself. Heracles had to think quickly. He pretended to be willing to swap places with Atlas, but asked the Titan to take the weight for a moment so that he could settle it more comfortably. Atlas did so, and Heracles made his escape.

12. To bring Cerberus from Tartarus

Cerberus was a monstrous, three-headed dog who guarded the gates of the Underworld and prevented anyone leaving the land of the dead. **Pluto** gave Heracles permission to take Cerberus as long as he did not use any weapons. The hero had to drag the struggling animal all the way to the court of Eurystheus.

Other adventures

Heracles had many other adventures. On one journey he killed the eagle that tormented **Prometheus** and freed him (see pages 20-21). He sailed with the **Argonauts** (see pages 32-33) and also freed **Theseus** from his chains in the Underworld (see page 36). He still suffered fits of madness sent by Hera, until he was finally cured by the witch, **Medea**.

The death of Heracles

Heracles later married **Deianeira** and they had several children, but Hera finally caused his death. She tricked Deianeira into giving Heracles a magic robe. She told her the magic would keep Heracles faithful to her, but in fact it was poisoned. The shirt caused agony when he put it on and he could not remove it. He had a funeral pyre built and climbed on it to die and escape the pain. **Zeus** snatched his son from the fire and took him to Mount Olympus, where he became an Immortal.

PARIS, HELEN AND TROY

The 'real' Troy

According to **Homer**, the great city of Troy stood in a commanding position overlooking the Hellespont. At the end of the nineteenth century, a German businessman called Heinrich Schliemann, who passionately believed that Homer's poem was a true account of an actual event, set out to prove that Troy had actually existed. Following clues in Homer, he explored the area and, in 1870, found the ruins of several cities, one on top of the other, just where Homer had said. Experts disagree about which layer of ruins might be Homer's Troy, but it seems clear that it was a real place.

This map shows the position of Troy and the other main places mentioned in the story of the Trojan War.

Actual wars?

The story of the Trojan Wars probably arose out of an actual war between the Greeks and Trojans. It seems likely that the Hittites, who had an established empire in what is now Turkey, encouraged Troy to thwart the ambitious Greeks' attempts to expand their trade and influence into the Black Sea area.

Greece and Troy were traditional rivals, according to legend. Their quarrelling finally led to a long and bitter war. It started with the love story of **Paris** and **Helen**, which you can read about below.

Paris

Paris was the son of King **Priam** and Queen **Hecuba** of Troy. At his birth it was predicted that he would cause the downfall of Troy so he was left on a hill to die. He was saved by a she-bear who fed him her milk until he was found by a herdsman who cared for him.

The judgement of Paris

This story starts at the wedding of **Thetis** and **Peleus** (page 23). It tells how **Eris**, the goddess of spite, took her revenge for not being invited.

Eris arrived during the feast with an apple inscribed, "For the fairest." **Hera, Athene** and **Aphrodite** all reached for it. **Zeus** did not want to choose between them, imagining the fury of the two not chosen. He decided someone else must judge and picked Paris.

Paris was guarding his foster-father's sheep when **Hermes** arrived with the goddesses and asked Paris to choose the loveliest.

Each goddess tried to bribe Paris: Hera with power and wealth; Athene with great victories and wisdom; but Aphrodite just smiled and promised him the love of the most beautiful woman in the world if he chose her. Paris could not resist Aphrodite and gave her the apple, earning the hatred of Hera and Athene.

Aphrodite said that the most beautiful woman in the world was Helen and that she lived in Greece at the court of **Menelaus** of Sparta. She did not say that Helen was Menelaus's wife.

Paris returns to Troy

Soon after, Paris competed in some Games in Troy and won more prizes than any Trojan prince. Afraid that someone might harm Paris out of jealousy, his foster-father revealed who he really was. The Trojans welcomed him, forgetting the prophesy.

Helen

Helen's parents were Zeus and **Leda** (see page 23). All the Greek princes wanted to marry

her. Her foster-father, **Tyndareus**, cleverly made all the suitors swear to support the man picked as her husband, then chose Menelaus.

Earlier, the Greeks had kidnapped Princess **Hesione** of Troy, Priam's sister. Priam sent Paris with some men to arrange her release and agreed that if the Greeks did not comply, they would seize a Greek princess in return.

Helen had never loved Menelaus, and when Paris came to Sparta she fell in love with him, as Aphrodite had promised. She agreed to run off with him, so the Trojans returned with a Greek princess as planned.

Menelaus was furious when Helen disappeared. He knew she had left willingly and that his own men had started the trouble by kidnapping Hesione, but he could not accept the insult. He asked his brother, **Agamemnon**, and Helen's former suitors to help get her back.

The suitors

Many of the suitors did not want to go to war, despite their promise to support Helen's husband. One, **Odysseus**, pretended to be mad when Menelaus's men came to fetch him. He started ploughing the beach but they placed his baby son, **Telemachus**, in his path and Odysseus swerved, proving he was sane.

At last, a thousand ships were prepared and armed to go to war against Troy.

The Trojans were willing to go to war for Helen because she had charmed them all. Only **Cassandra**, Paris's sister, predicted disaster. She could see the future, but had displeased **Apollo**, who cursed her never to be believed.

Eris's revenge

The Greek fleet was held up for lack of wind and this was when Agamemnon sacrificed his daughter, **Iphigenia** (see page 17). The wind changed at last and they sailed to Troy. The Trojans would not return Helen so the war, which was Eris's spiteful revenge, began.

THE TROJAN WAR

The war dragged on for ten years. The Greeks could not break into Troy and the Trojans could not drive them off.

Aeneas

Many heroes were killed on both sides. One great Trojan hero was **Aeneas, Aphrodite's** son by **Anchises**. He was wounded by **Diomedes** and Aphrodite rushed to help him. Diomedes stopped her and even dared graze her with his spear. In the end, Apollo carried him to **Leto** and **Artemis**, who healed him.

Achilles

The most famous Greek warrior was **Achilles**. He was one of the seven sons of **Thetis** and **Peleus**. She made six of her sons immortal by burning away their mortal half. She was doing the same for the baby Achilles, when Peleus came in. He thought she was hurting the child and prevented her finishing, so Achilles was left with one vulnerable place on his body where he could be fatally wounded – the heel by which Thetis had held him.

Achilles was given the choice of a long, undistinguished life or a short but glorious one. He chose the second.

As time went on, the warriors began to quarrel. Achilles argued with **Agamemnon** over a slave girl and left the battle, sulking. The Greeks lost heart and were driven back by the Trojan hero **Hector, Priam's** son.

The deaths of three heroes

In desperation **Patroclus** put on Achilles's armour and led an attack. He was not as skilled as Achilles, though, the Trojans saw through his disguise and Hector killed him. Achilles was stricken with guilt and sorrow and plunged back into battle. He killed Hector and dragged his body round the city behind his chariot before letting the Trojans buy it back for burial.

Paris emerged to avenge Hector's death and shot Achilles in the heel – his only weak spot – and killed him.

Ajax kills himself

Ajax and **Odysseus** disputed who should inherit Achilles's armour, as they had both guarded his body during the battle. Agamemnon decided Odysseus should have it and Ajax killed himself in shame. To prevent more trouble, Odysseus gave the armour to Achilles's son **Neoptolemus**.

With many of their heroes dead, the Greeks were told that only the famous archer **Philoctetes** could save them.

Philoctetes brings new hope

Philoctetes had been on his way to Troy when he was bitten by a snake. His wound was not fatal, but would not heal, so the Greeks had left him behind. He felt very bitter about this treatment and when the Greeks came back to beg for his help he refused at first. Then **Heracles** came to him in a dream, saying that if he forgave the Greeks and went to Troy, his wound would heal. He returned with them and killed Paris with a skillful shot, which gave the Greeks new hope. At once the snake bite began to heal as Heracles had promised.

The Trojan horse

Troy finally fell thanks to a trick thought up by Odysseus. The Greeks pretended to give up. They built a huge wooden horse as a gift to **Athene**, so she would grant them a safe trip home. They left it outside the gates of Troy and sailed away. The Trojans were overjoyed. They pulled the horse through the city gates and offered it at their own temple of Athene.

That night they celebrated, but when they were all asleep, some Greeks who had hidden inside the hollow horse slipped out of the trapdoor in its side. They opened the city gates to let in the Greek army, who had sneaked back under cover of darkness.

The Greeks ransacked Troy and vast numbers of Trojans were killed. **Helen** was captured and taken to **Menelaus**. He intended to punish her but despite all the bloodshed she had caused, he found he still loved her and took her back as his wife.

AFTER THE TROJAN WAR

The trick of the wooden horse (page 43) ended the Trojan War. **Paris** had caused the destruction of Troy, as predicted, and the surviving Greeks went home. But for some of the characters their adventures did not end with the war.

Aeneas and the Palladium

Aeneas was one of the few Trojan nobles who survived. He escaped from Troy with a sacred statue called the Palladium. It was a gift from **Athene** and it was said that wherever it stood would be the centre of a great empire.

After many travels Aeneas settled in Italy. His descendants were supposed to have been present at the founding of Rome and to have placed the Palladium in a Roman temple. Rome did become the capital of an empire and Julius Caesar claimed descent from Aeneas and his mother, Venus (**Aphrodite's** Roman name).

Agamemnon's return

Agamemnon was a descendant of **Tantalus** (see page 27), and was thus subject to **Zeus's** curse on his family. The fates of Agamemnon and his son, **Orestes**, illustrate the Greeks' belief in retribution, by which you reaped the rewards or punishments of your own behaviour, or that of your ancestors.

After the war, Agamemnon went home to Mycenae where his wife, **Clytemnestra**, was waiting for him. She hated Agamemnon. He had killed her first husband and married her by force. He sacrificed their daughter, **Iphigenia**, for a favourable wind to go to war (Clytemnestra did not know about the rescue by **Artemis** – see page 17) and then stayed away fighting for ten years. Clytemnestra plotted her revenge with Agamemnon's cousin, **Aegisthus**, who had always wanted to be king himself.

Agamemnon brought **Cassandra** (see page 41) home with him as a slave. She had already given birth to his twin sons and when Clytemnestra saw them she was even more determined to punish her husband.

Pretending to welcome him home, Clytemnestra offered the weary Agamemnon a hot bath. He accepted, paying no attention to Cassandra's warnings of danger which, as usual, were not believed. When he had taken off his clothes and armour and was defenceless, Clytemnestra stabbed him to death. She killed Cassandra and her twins, too, and married Aegisthus. They ruled as king and queen and seemed to have got away with their crimes.

Orestes and the Oracle

Clytemnestra and Agamemnon had children other than Iphigenia. Their son, **Orestes**, was being brought up at his grandparents' home, so he did not witness the murder of his father. Their daughter, **Electra**, was not so lucky. She had to live with the murderess and her new husband and watch them do well.

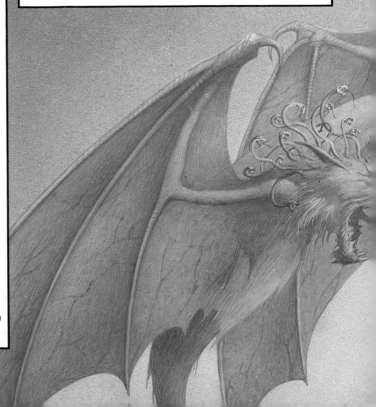

When he grew older, Orestes received a command from the Delphic **Oracle** to avenge his father's death. He was horrified, but went home with his cousin, **Pylades**, to find out what was going on.

Electra soon convinced him that their mother was guilty and should be punished. Spurred on by her hatred, Orestes killed Clytemnestra and Aegisthus. Thus their evil deeds were punished.

Retribution

However, killing your mother, no matter what she had done, was the worst possible crime. The avenging **Furies** (see page 8) soon came hunting Orestes and drove him mad with grief and remorse. It was no excuse that **Apollo** himself had ordered the murder through his Oracle.

Orestes was driven to wandering through Greece. In Sparta he tried to kill **Helen** as she had caused so much misery but Zeus came down, wrapped her in a cloud and took her to Olympus to be a goddess.

In Athens Orestes begged to be put on trial. Athene was the judge and Apollo himself appeared to defend Orestes. Athene decided Orestes had suffered enough and ordered the Furies to leave him alone. Three of them did so but the rest continued to pursue him.

The Oracle next told Orestes to sail to the land of the Taurians and bring back a statue of Artemis they had. The Taurians were barbarians who sacrificed strangers but Orestes and Pylades set off anyway. They were captured and prepared for sacrifice but when the priestess came to kill them, it was Iphigenia. She had been brought there by Artemis when she was saved from death. She recognized her brother and helped him and Pylades escape with the statue.

The curse is lifted

At last Orestes had made amends for his crime, the curse on his family was lifted and he was left in peace. Iphigenia continued as a priestess of Artemis, Pylades married Electra and Orestes married **Hermione**, daughter of Helen and **Menelaus**.

THE ADVENTURES OF ODYSSEUS

Odysseus lived on the island of Ithaca with his wife, **Penelope**, and son, **Telemachus**. He had been warned that if he went to Troy he would not return for twenty years. He tried to avoid going (see page 41) but it was no use, as he had sworn to help **Menelaus**.

The Odyssey
Odysseus fought at Troy for ten years, and it was his idea for the wooden horse that ended the war. His journey home was full of mishaps, which were recounted in **Homer's** poem, The Odyssey.

First, his ship was separated from the rest in a storm. It was washed up in the land of the **Lotus-eaters** (Libya). Eating lotus-fruit made you forget everything except the desire to eat more fruit. Some sailors succumbed and had to be dragged back to the ship.

They called at the island of the **Cyclops**, **Polyphemus**, who shut them in a cave with his sheep and began to eat them one by one.

The sheep went out to graze each morning but the giant never let a man slip out, too. Eventually, Odysseus found a stick and used it to blind Polyphemus while he slept. When the sheep went out next morning, the men clung to their bellies. The blind Cyclops felt each sheep to make sure no-one escaped on their backs, but did not think to feel underneath them. When he discovered the trick, Polyphemus asked **Poseidon** to avenge him.

Not long after, the crew were entertained by **Aeolus**, guardian of the winds (see page 48). He tied the storm winds in a bag and gave them to Odysseus to keep. His foolish men thought the bag contained treasure and opened it, releasing a tempest.

They were driven onto Aeaea, home of **Circe**, a witch. She turned unwanted visitors into pigs and this was the fate of the first men sent for help by Odysseus. **Hermes** gave Odysseus a flower that made him immune to Circe's spells. He demanded the release of his men. Circe was impressed by his boldness and fell in love with him. She restored his men and they stayed with her for a while. She had three sons with Odysseus, though he remained keen to go home.

Circe sent him to the Underworld to consult **Tiresias** (see page 15) about his future. The seer warned him that when he got home he would find men fighting over his goods.

They finally left Aeaea, sailing safely past the **sirens** (see page 33) by blocking their ears with wax, except for Odysseus who wanted to hear their voices. He had himself tied to the mast so he could not be lured to them.

Still the dangers were not over. They had to negotiate a narrow channel between two monsters it was almost impossible to avoid. One was the **Scylla**, who had six heads and snapping dogs at her waist. The other was the whirlpool **Charybdis** which sucked ships to their doom. Odysseus chose to pass nearer the Scylla and just got by, though she killed some of his men.

On Sicily the sailors killed and ate some of the cattle of the **Titan, Hyperion**. Tiresias had warned Odysseus not to harm these sacred animals and the angry gods sank his ship, drowning all the men. Odysseus survived by clinging to the mast.

He was washed up on the island of Ortygia, where **Thetis's** daughter, **Calypso**, ruled. She stopped Odysseus leaving for seven years until Zeus sent Hermes to make her let him go.

At last he reached the shores of Ithaca and entered his court disguised as an old man.

He found things as Tiresias had predicted. The nobles were squandering his wealth and trying to make Penelope re-marry. She knew that if Odysseus was dead it would be wise to accept one of them but she delayed choosing, claiming she must finish her weaving first. She wove all day, then undid her work at night. This ruse was eventually discovered and she was forced to complete the cloth.

Odysseus revealed his true identity to his son, Telemachus, and they secretly removed all the nobles' weapons from the hall.

Penelope said she would marry the man who could string the bow Odysseus had left behind and shoot an arrow. She was sure no-one could do it. The suitors tried but failed. Odysseus then came forward. They laughed at the "old man" but he easily strung the bow and shot an arrow. Realizing who he must be, they reached for their weapons, only to find they were gone. Odysseus had no pity and killed them all.

Odysseus settled down again with his family, but one day a strange ship arrived. Odysseus attacked, thinking they were raiders. He was killed in the fight and only afterwards was it discovered that the strangers were led by his own son, one of Circe's children.

MORE HEROES

There are many more heroes and stories which there has not been room to include – some of them are briefly mentioned here.

Aeolus, keeper of the winds

Aeolus was keeper of the winds. He was supposed to let them loose one at a time but they were often hard to control. The **East Wind, Eurus**, was violent and disorderly; **Boreas**, the **North Wind** (see page 30), was cold and blustery; **Auster** was the hot, rainy **South Wind** and the gentle **West Wind** was called **Zephyr**.

Handsome humans

The gods sometimes picked out especially attractive humans as friends. Here are the stories of two of them:

Ganymede, the son of King **Tros** of Troy, was a very handsome youth. **Zeus** sent an eagle to pluck him from Earth to become an Immortal on Olympus. He took over as cup-bearer to the gods from the goddess, **Hebe**, and his image was placed among the stars as **Aquarius**, the water-carrier.

Hyacinthus was a Spartan prince. He was also strikingly good-looking and became **Apollo's** companion. The West Wind was jealous of their friendship and when Apollo was teaching Hyacinthus to throw the discus, the wind caught up the heavy disc and flung it back at the prince, killing him. Where his blood fell the first hyacinth flowers grew.

Creon

Creon drove **Oedipus** from Thebes, took the crown and became king in his place. Oedipus's sons rebelled, but were killed. Creon forbade them proper burial, which meant their spirits could not find peace. Their sister, **Antigone**, secretly sought their bodies and performed the burial ceremony. Creon condemned her to death, but his own son, **Haemon**, saved and married her.

Hellen

Hellen was the son of **Deucalion** and grandson of **Prometheus**. The Greeks claimed him as their ancestor, calling themselves Hellenes. There were four Hellenic races: Aeolians, from **Aeolus**, Hellen's eldest son; Dorians, from **Dorus**, his youngest; Ionians and Achaeans from his grandsons, **Ion** and **Achaeus**.

Aristaeus

He was the bee-keeping son of Apollo and the water-nymph, **Cyrene**. He made advances to **Orpheus's** wife, **Eurydice**, and she was running away from him when she received her fatal snake bite (see page 31). As punishment for causing her death, his bees died and he had to make sacrifices to Orpheus and Eurydice to make amends.

Aristaeus was the father of **Actaeon**, who was torn to pieces by **Artemis's** hounds (see page 17). After his son's death he travelled to Sardinia, Sicily and Thrace, where he was worshipped as a god.

Arion

Legend says that **Arion's** father was **Poseidon** and his mother a **nymph**, though he may have been based on a real poet. He was a skilled musician and in one contest he won so many prizes that, on his way home, some sailors threw him overboard, meaning to steal his treasure. Luckily, his playing had attracted several dolphins and one of them took Arion on his back and swam him safely home.

Daedalus

Daedalus was a craftsman at King **Minos's** court. He was a noble Athenian but had fled Greece after murdering someone. He later offended Minos and was imprisoned. His escape is described on page 26.

Hoping to recapture Daedalus, Minos issued a challenge: that no-one could pass a linen thread through a Triton shell. It was almost impossible, as the shells have spiral insides. Minos knew that if anyone could do it, Daedalus could and he was right. Daedalus tied the thread to an ant, which he sent through the shell, drawing the thread behind it. He was not recaptured, though.

Calchas

Calchas was a Trojan who joined the Greeks against his own countrymen. He was a great seer and predicted many of the events in the Trojan Wars. He is supposed to have died of humiliation when he met **Mopsus**, a seer wiser than himself.

Pelops

Pelops was the unfortunate son that **Tantalus** served to the gods for dinner (see page 27). The gods punished Tantalus and brought Pelops back to life, giving him an ivory shoulder to replace the one **Demeter** had absent-mindedly chewed.

Pelops wanted to marry **Hippodamia,** daughter of King **Oenomaus**. The king had been told he would be killed by his son-in-law so he challenged suitors to a chariot race in which the loser was executed. No-one had yet beaten him, but Poseidon lent Pelops some winged horses, while Pelops bribed the charioteer **Myrtilus** to sabotage the king's chariot.

Oenomaus was killed in a huge crash. Pelops, his bride and Myrtilus escaped, but Pelops ungratefully threw Myrtilus into the sea. This renewed the curse which Tantalus had earned for his family, and it was passed on to his grandson, **Agamemnon**. It was only lifted by his great-grandson, **Orestes** (see pages 44-45).

Cadmus

Cadmus was **Europa's** brother (see page 22). He went looking for her after Zeus stole her away and had many adventures. Once, he killed a serpent of Apollo's, as it had slain his men. **Athene** told him to plant the serpent's teeth and when he did, armed warriors sprang up. Cadmus set them fighting each other and when there were only five left alive he took them into his service to replace his men.

WHO'S WHO IN THE GREEK MYTHS

This section is a Who's Who of characters and monsters in the Greek myths. Any character whose name appears in bold type in this book has an entry here and there are some extra entries that do not appear in these stories but which you may come across elsewhere. The

Who's Who tells you about the family, doings, personality, appearance and magic powers of each character. It is arranged alphabetically and some abbreviations have been used to save space. You can find out how to understand the entries in the example below.

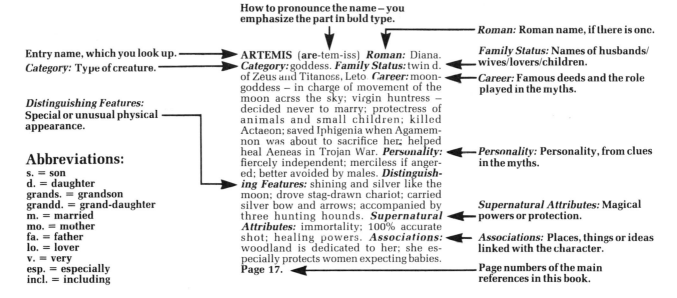

How to pronounce the name – you emphasize the part in bold type.

Roman: Roman name, if there is one.

Entry name, which you look up.
Category: Type of creature.

ARTEMIS (**are**-tem-iss) *Roman:* Diana. *Category:* goddess. *Family Status:* twin d. of Zeus and Titaness, Leto. *Career:* moon-goddess – in charge of movement of the moon acrss the sky; virgin huntress – decided never to marry; protectress of animals and small children; killed Actaeon; saved Iphigenia when Agamemnon was about to sacrifice her; helped heal Aeneas in Trojan War. *Personality:* fiercely independent; merciless if angered; better avoided by males. *Distinguishing Features:* shining and silver like the moon; drove stag-drawn chariot; carried silver bow and arrows; accompanied by three hunting hounds. *Supernatural Attributes:* immortality; 100% accurate shot; healing powers. *Associations:* woodland is dedicated to her; she especially protects women expecting babies. **Page 17.**

Family Status: Names of husbands/wives/lovers/children.

Career: Famous deeds and the role played in the myths.

Distinguishing Features: Special or unusual physical appearance.

Personality: Personality, from clues in the myths.

Supernatural Attributes: Magical powers or protection.

Associations: Places, things or ideas linked with the character.

Page numbers of the main references in this book.

Abbreviations:

s. = son
d. = daughter
grands. = grandson
grandd. = grand-daughter
m. = married
mo. = mother
fa. = father
lo. = lover
v. = very
esp. = especially
incl. = including

ACAMAS (**ak**-a-mass) *Category:* mortal. *Family Status:* s. of Theseus and Phaedra; lo. of Phyllis (relationship tragically ended before marriage due to her broken heart). *Career:* military hero; was one of the soldiers who hid in the Trojan horse. *Personality:* career-minded, to the detriment of his personal life; faithful. **Page 30.**

ACHAEUS (a-**kee**-us) see **HELLEN.**

ACHILLES (a-**kill**-eez) *Category:* mortal. *Family Status:* s. of Peleus and Thetis; lo. of Deidameia; one s. Neoptolemus. *Career:* hero; chose glorious life and early death; important (if erratic) military commander for Greeks in Trojan War; abandoned battle at crucial point, but returned for vengeance when his friend, Patroclus, was killed; slew Hector; received fatal wound in heel from Paris. *Personality:* v. brave and eager to excell in battle; jealous of his position; staunch friend when roused; fond of women; prone to moodiness and sulking. *Distinguishing Features:* swift of foot. *Supernatural Attributes:* invulnerable to all weapons, except for one spot on his heel. *Associations:* someone's physical or emotional weak spot can be called his "Achilles' heel"; the tendon in your heel that joins your foot to your calf is called the "Achilles' tendon". **Page 42.**

ACRISIUS (a-**kriss**-ee-us) *Category:* mortal. *Family Status:* nephew of

Hyacinthus; one d. Danae; one grands. Perseus. *Career:* king; blighted by prophecy that he would be killed by his grands.; set Danae and baby Perseus adrift on the sea but could not avoid Fate; was killed accidentally by Perseus. during a discus-throwing contest. **Page 22.**

ACTAEON (act-**ee**-on) *Category:* mortal. *Family Status:* s. of Aristaeus. *Career:* successful huntsman; made rare sighting of Artemis bathing; she turned him into a stag and he was hunted and killed by his own hounds. *Personality:* inquisitive; rash. *Distinguishing Features:* excellent bowman. **Page 17.**

ADONIS (a-**don**-iss) *Category:* mortal. *Family Status:* lo. of Aphrodite; lo. of Persephone. *Career:* affairs with goddesses attracted unwelcome attention from jealous Ares; killed by Ares in disguise as a boar; thanks to Aphrodite's pleading, he spent summers on Earth with her. *Personality:* carefree; popular with women. *Associations:* anemone flowers sprang up where his blood fell. **Page 13.**

AEETES (aye-**ee**-teez) *Category:* mortal. *Family Status:* one s.; one d. Medea. *Career:* King of Colchis; obstructed Jason's quest for golden fleece; made attempt on Jason's life by asking him to harness fire-breathing bulls and plant dragon's teeth; gave chase when Jason left

with fleece; persecution of Jason ended by brutal murder of his s. by Medea. *Personality:* sly; cunning. **Page 32.**

AEGEUS (ij-**ee**-us) *Category:* mortal. *Family Status:* one s. Theseus (by magic); m. Medea; one s. *Career:* King of Athens; drove Medea away after she tried to poison Theseus; early misfortune in being responsible for death of King Minos's son led to terrible debt – 7 young men and 7 girls sent to Crete every 9 years to be sacrificed to the Minotaur; drowned himself soon after seeing Theseus's ship return from Crete with black sails raised, the sign that Theseus was dead. *Personality:* anxious; depressive. *Associations:* place where he drowned named Aegean Sea after him. **Page 34**

AEGISTHUS (ee-**giss**-thus) *Category:* mortal. *Family Status:* cousin of Agamemnon; m. Clytemnestra (unlawfully, as she had been m. to Agamemnon and it was not permitted to marry such a close relative's former husband or wife). *Career:* quarrelled with Agamemnon over throne of Mycenae; became king by criminal means – accomplice in murder of Agamemnon; executed by his step-s., Orestes. *Personality:* heartless, bitter and ambitious. **Page 44.**

AEGYPTUS (ee-**jip**-tus) *Category:* mortal. *Family Status:* grands. of Poseidon; 50 s. *Career:* famous for attempted mass-murder of his brother, Danaus, and Danaus's 50 daughters; plot foiled by proposed victims. *Personality:* greedy, cruel. *Associations:* Egypt named after him. **Page 25.**

AENEAS (in-**ee**-us) *Category:* mortal. *Family Status:* s. of Anchises and Aphrodite; lo. of Dido. *Career:* great hero; warrior for Troy in Trojan War; wounded by Diomedes, healed by Leto and Artemis; escaped fall of Troy with his fa. and small son; fled to Italy with Palladium; descendants founded Rome; doomed love affair with Dido, whom he abandoned. *Personality:* tremendous courage tempered by survival instinct. *Supernatural Attributes:* enjoys special protection of his mo., Aphrodite. **Pages 42, 44,**

AEOLUS (ee-**ole**-us) *Category:* god *Family Status:* fa. of Alcyone. *Career:* keeper of the winds; gave captured storm winds to·Odysseus in a bag so he would only have fair winds. *Personality:* generally helpful, but not always able to control his charges. *Supernatural Attributes:* immortality. *Associations:* Aeolian Islands (NW of Sicily) named after him; Aeolian harp – instrument with strings which make music when wind blows across them. **Pages 46, 48.**

AGAMEMNON (ag-a-**mem**non) *Category:* mortal. *Family Status:* descendant of Atreus; m. Clytemnestra by force; one s. Orestes; three d. Electra, Iphigenia, Chrysothemis; brother of Menelaus. *Career;* King of Mycenae; soldier; commander of Greek troops in Trojan War; sacrificed Iphigenia; quarrelled with Achilles; took Cassandra slave; assassinated by Clytemnestra. *Personality:* violent and aggressive; argumentative; ruthless, even to his family; tactless. *Associations:* Heinrich Schliemann (see p. 40) thought he had found gold mask of Agamemnon amongst treasures at Mycenae – it actually turned out to be much older. **Page 44.**

AGAVE (a-**garv**-ee) *Category:* mortal. *Family Status:* mo. of Pentheus. *Career:* Queen of Thebes; Maenad (worshipper of Dionysus); killed Pentheus while under influence of religious trance. *Personality:* religious fanatic; best avoided, espcially by men, during religious ceremonies. *Supernatural Attributes:* superhuman strength in religious-induced frenzy; aid from Dionysus. **Page 19.**

AJAX (**age**-axe) *Category:* mortal. *Career:* mighty hero for Greeks in Trojan War; quarrelled with Odysseus over Achilles's armour; wasteful death by suicide. *Personality:* very strong but not too bright; obsessed with honour. **Page 42.**

ALCMENE (alk-**meen**-ee) *Category:* mortal. *Family Status:* m. Amphitryon; unwilling lo. of Zeus; one s. Heracles (fa. Zeus). *Career:* faithful wife, until tricked by Zeus. *Personality:* loyal. **Page 23.**

AMAZONS (am-a-zonz) *Category:* mortals. *Family Status:* descended from Ares and a naiad; do not generally marry, but have children by arrangement, involving no ties to the father. *Career:* fierce warriors; supported Troy in Trojan War; prevented Heracles taking their queen's girdle and he had to fight all of them. *Personalities:* ferocious; excellent shots. *Distinguishing Features:* female race; sometimes said to cut right breast off for ease of pulling bowstring; lived near the Black Sea. **Page 36.**

AMPHITRITE (am-fee-**try**-tee) *Category:* demi-goddess; nereid. *Family Status:* m. Poseidon; three children. *Career:* support to Poseidon; turned Scylla into a monster. *Distinguishing Features:* encountered by the sea. *Personality:* jealous. **Page 11.**

ANCHISES (an-**kye**-seez) *Category:* mortal. *Family Status:* lo. of Aphrodite; one s. Aeneas. *Career:* King of Dardanians; revealed his affair with Aphrodite so punished by Zeus. *Personality:* unable to keep a secret. *Distinguishing Features:* v. handsome. **Page 13.**

ANDROMEDA (an-**drom**-med-a) *Category:* mortal. *Family Status:* d. of King of Ethiopia; m. Perseus. *Career:* princess; her foolish parents boasted she was lovelier than the nereids; to appease Poseidon she was chained to a rock as sacrifice to a sea-monster; dramatic rescue in nick of time by Perseus. *Personality:* obedient, innocent. *Distinguishing Features:* beautiful as the nereids (almost). **Page 24.**

ANTIGONE (an-**tig**-on-ee) *Category:* mortal. *Family Status:* d. of Oedipus and Jocasta; lo. of Haemon. *Career:* acted as guide to Oedipus after he blinded himself; searched for and buried her brothers' bodies when killed in battle; condemned to death by Creon; hanged herself; Haemon stabbed himself when he found her dead. *Personality:* noble, brave and self-sacrificing; great loyalty to family and duty. **Pages 29, 48.**

APHRODITE (aff-ro-**die**-tee) *Roman:* Venus. *Category:* goddess. *Family Status:* d. of Uranus – born from foam caused by his blood dropping in the Ocean; m. Hephaestos; lo. of Ares; lo. of Anchises; lo. of Adonis and others; two s. Eros (fa. Ares?), Aeneas (fa. Anchises); one d. Harmonia (fa. Ares). *Career:* goddess of love; no formal duties except being lovely; competitive with Hera and Athene; responsible for Trojan War, as she promised Helen to Paris if he judged her fairest of the goddesses; fought for Troy in Trojan War, although it was unusual for her to take part in warfare; was wounded by Diomedes; brought about death of Adonis by arguing with Persephone over him and rousing Ares's jealousy; caused death of Glaucus by driving his horses mad; brought the statue, Galatea, to life for Pygmalion for his loyalty to true love. *Personality:* irresistibly charming; large appetite for lovers but fickle in affections; vain and competitive about her beauty. *Distinguishing Features:* exceeding beauty; usually accompanied by doves and sparrows, her special birds. *Supernatural Attributes:* immortality; girdle which makes everyone fall in love with the wearer – can be lent to humans. *Associations:* she was closely associated with Cyprus where she arrived soon after she was born. **Pages 12, 13.**

APOLLO (a-**poll**-o) *Category:* god. *Family Status:* twin s. of Zeus and Titaness, Leto; lo. of Calliope, the Muse; lo. of Coronis; lo. of Cyrene and others; three s. Orpheus (mo. Calliope), Asclepius (mo. Coronis), Aristaeus (mo. Cyrene). *Career:* sun god – in charge of the sun's movement across the sky; hunter; god and patron of the Arts – skilled musician on the lyre; tamed the Muses; killed the Python; famous for Oracles, prophecies told through his priests and priestesses; killed Marsyas after music contest; chased Daphne unsuccessfully. *Personality:* proud; protective towards his mother and sister; artistic; could be cruel. *Distinguishing Features:* carries gold bow and arrows; appears gold and shining, like the sun; wears laurel wreath in memory of Daphne. *Supernatural Attributes:* immortality; healing powers. *Associations:* small groups of trees were sacred to him; the raven was his bird. **Page 16.**

AQUARIUS (a-**kware**-ee-us) see **GANYMEDE.**

ARACHNE (a-**rack**-nee) *Category:* mortal. *Career:* skilled weaver; cut short in her prime by foolish boasting that she wove better than Athene; driven to suicide to avoid Athene's wrath; was turned into a spider so her spinning skill would not be lost. *Personality:* highly-skilled but thoughtless. *Distinguishing Features:* expert web-weaving after transformation. **Page 15.**

ARES (**are**-eez) *Roman:* Mars. *Category:* god. *Family Status:* s. of Zeus and Hera; twin sister, Eris; lo. of Aphrodite; one s. Eros (mo. Aphrodite); one d. Harmonia (mo. Aphrodite). *Career:* god of war; involvement in all war-like activities, regardless of merit; will intervene on opposing sides if possible; took the shape of a boar and killed Adonis. *Personality:* violent and eager for a fight; revels in bloodshed; undependable ally as indifferent to the rights and wrongs of a dispute; expert but jealous lover (according to Aphrodite). *Distinguishing Features:* young, strong and handsome; preference for battle-gear. *Supernatural Attributes:* immortality; shape-changing. *Associations:* the Areopagus (Hill of Ares), situated NW of the Acropolis (Athens), was location for important trials. **Page 12.**

ARGONAUTS (**are**-go-norts) *Category:* mortals. *Family Status:* varied, but mostly noble. *Career:* many of them did other famous deeds but all were members of crew of Jason's ship, Argo; sailed with Jason on quest for golden fleece; drove off the Harpies; negotiated Clashing Rocks; resisted singing of Sirens; helped kill Talos. *Personalities:* tough; hungry for glory. *Distinguishing Features:* heavily armed. **Page 32.**

ARGUS (**are**-gus) *Category:* monster. *Family Status:* Hera's servant. *Career:* doing Hera's bidding; set to guard Io; killed Echidne; lulled to sleep and killed by Hermes. *Distinguishing Features:* 100 eyes, never all closed at once. *Associations:* after·his death, Hera set his eyes in tail of the peacock, which became her symbol. **Page 22.**

ARIADNE (a-ree-**add**-nee) *Category:* mortal. *Family Status:* d. of Minos and Pasiphae; lo. of Theseus; m. Dionysus; six s. *Career:* Cretan princess; helped Theseus kill Minotaur; left Crete with him; abandoned by him on Naxos; rescued by and m. Dionysus; called down punishment on Theseus for abandoning her – caused death of his father, Aegeus. *Personality:* daring; vengeful; passionate. **Page 36.**

ARION (a-rye-on) *Category:* mortal. *Career:* musician; made good living by playing lyre; won many contests; was mugged for his winnings by some sailors; saved by dolphins. *Personality:* easy-going, lucky. **Page 49.**

ARISTAEUS (a-riss-**tay**-us) *Category:* demi-god. *Family Status:* s. of Apollo and water-nymph, Cyrene; three s. incl. Actaeon; one d. *Career:* bee-keeper; chased Eurydice to her death in the woods; as punishment, the gods made his bees die until he made sacrifices to atone; travelled widely after death of Actaeon and worshipped as a god. *Personality:* persistent; insensitive. *Supernatural Attributes:* immortality.

ARTEMIS (**are**-tem-iss) *Roman:* Diana. *Category:* goddess. *Family Status:* twin d. of Zeus and Titaness, Leto. *Career:* moon-goddess – in charge of movement of the moon acrss the sky; virgin huntress – decided never to marry; protectress of animals and small children; killed Actaeon; saved Iphigenia when Agamemnon was about to sacrifice her; helped heal Aeneas in Trojan War. *Personality:* fiercely independent; merciless if angered; better avoided by males. *Distinguishing Features:* shining and silver like the moon; drove stag-drawn chariot; carried silver bow and arrows; accompanied by three hunting hounds. *Supernatural Attributes:* immortality; 100% accurate shot; healing powers. *Associations:* woodland is dedicated to her; she especially protects women expecting babies. **Page 17.**

ASCLEPIUS (ass-**kleep**-ee-us) *Category:* god. *Family Status:* s. of Apollo and Coronis; two s; four d. incl. Panacea, Hygieia. . *Career:* god of medicine; v. successful doctor; went too far by bringing the dead back to life; killed by Zeus, then revived by him to become an Immortal. *Personality:* compassionate; proud of his powers, leading to showing-off; not respectful enough of the gods. *Supernatural Attributes:* immortality; healing powers, learnt from Apollo. *Associations:* his symbol – snakes twisted round a staff – became the symbol of pharmacy in many countries. **Page 16.**

ATHAMAS (**ath**-a-mass) *Category:* mortal. *Family Status:* m. Nephele, the cloud-woman; two s. incl. Phrixus; one d. Helle; m. Ino. *Career:* king; happy reign with Nephele but made big mistake when he put Nephele aside for Ino; tricked by Ino into sacrificing Phrixus – lost both his children by this act. *Personality:* good-natured but gullible. **Page 25.**

ATHENE (a-**thee**-nee) *Roman:* Minerva. *Category:* goddess. *Family Status:* d. of Zeus; born from his head, after he swallowed Titaness Metis in form of a fly; virgin goddess, never married *Career:* goddess of wisdom and war; preferred reason to violence, except when pushed; better warrior even than Ares; arbitrator of disputes; overseer of home crafts; inventor of flute; created olive tree and gave it to Greeks; blinded Tiresias, but gave him second sight to compensate; turned Medusa into a monster; turned Arachne into a spider for boasting she could weave better than her. *Personality:* v. wise; slow to anger, but highly dangerous if roused; competitive with other gods and humans. *Distinguishing Features:* always wore armour – especially noted for her helmet; carried Zeus's shield, the aegis; often called grey-eyed or flashing-eyed. *Supernatural Attributes:* unbeatable in combat; immortality. *Associations:* the owl is her bird; Athens named after her; also called Athene Parthenos and Pallas Athene. **Pages 14, 15.**

ATLAS (at-lass). *Category:* Titan. *Family Status:* s. of Uranus and Mother Earth; m. Hesperis, several d., the Hesperides. *Career:* one of the rulers of the world, under Uranus, until revolt of Zeus and the New Gods; fought with Uranus against Zeus; defeated, and punished by being made to support the heavens on his shoulders; almost escaped when he persuaded Heracles to take the weight while he went to fetch golden apples from his daughters, but was tricked into taking it back; turned to stone when shown Gorgon's head by Perseus. *Personality:* not too bright. *Distinguishing Features:* physical giant; massive strength. *Associations:* Atlas Mountains in Africa said to be where he was turned to stone.

AUGEUS (awe-**jee**-us) *Category:* mortal. *Career:* reputation based solely on filthiness of his stables, which had to be cleaned as one of the Twelve Labours of Heracles. *Personality:* uncaring to animals; slack in hygiene. **Page 39.**

AUSTER (**oss**-ter). *Category:* god. *Family Status:* kept in a bag, in the care of Aeolus. *Career:* South Wind; blew when and where released by Aeolus. *Personality:* hot and rainy. *Distinguishing Features:* body of a man; sometimes given a serpent's tail. *Supernatural Attributes:* immortality; flying like the wind. *Associations:* gave his name to Australia. **Page 48.**

BACCHAE (**back**-ee) See **MAENADS**.

BACCHUS (**back**-us) See **DIONYSUS**.

BELLEROPHON (bell-**air**-oh-fon) *Category:* mortal. *Family Status:* s. of Glaucus; grands. of Sisyphus. *Career:* served King Proteus of Argos; lost good reputation in scandal, although innocent; sent with letter demanding his own death to King of Lycia; made good impression and was not killed but asked to slay the Chimaera; gods lent him winged horse, Pegasus, and he succeeded; served King of Lycia faithfully; ruined promising career by attempting to fly to Olympus on Pegasus; struck down by Zeus. *Personality:* dashing and brave; responds well to adversity; cocksure and inclined to be over-confident. *Supernatural Attributes:* flying ability when he had the use of Pegasus. **Page 28.**

BOREAS (**bore**-ee-ass) *Category:* god. *Family Status:* in the care of Aeolus; m. Oreithyia *Career:* North Wind; blew as the gods directed; after marriage, special concern for city of Athens – scattered attacking Persian fleet. *Personality:* cold and blustery. *Distinguishing Features:* man's upper body, serpent's tail; sometimes winged and with two faces, looking forward and back. *Supernatural Attributes:* immortality. **Page 30.**

Boreas

BRONZE RACE *Category:* mortals. *Family Status:* created by Prometheus; forefathers of all humans. *Career:* their descendants were the heroes of Greek myths. *Personalities:* generally noble and good. *Distinguishing Features:* made in the image of the gods; first human-shaped life forms on Earth. **Page 20.**

CADMUS (**cad**-muss) *Category:* mortal. *Family Status:* brother of Europe; m. Harmonia; many children incl. d. Semele and Agave. *Career:* Phoenician prince and hero; life of enforced adventure while searching for Europa after she was carried off by Zeus; advised by Athene to plant serpent's teeth, from which sprang warriors which he took into his service; told by Oracle to follow a cow and found a city where it lay down; founded Thebes and ruled as king; went to Isles of the Blessed when he died. *Personality:* brave and dependable; good leader; inspired confidence. **Page 49.**

CALCHAS (**kal**-kass) *Category:* mortal. *Career:* seer and priest of Apollo; was Trojan but supported Greece in Trojan War; told future for Agamemnon; unusual death of mortification upon meeting Mopsus, a seer greater than himself. *Personality:* conscientious; proud of his powers; useful back-up to military commander; willing to be unpopular, as his predictions were often bad news. *Supernatural Attributes:* power to predict future events, given by Apollo. **Page 49.**

CALLISTO (cal-**iss**-toe) *Category:* demi-goddess; nymph *Family Status:* lo. of Zeus; one s. Arcas. *Career:* follower of Artemis; broke rules of chastity by falling in love with Zeus; turned into a bear by Artemis; hunted and killed; turned into star group, the Great Bear, by Zeus; Arcas was ancestor of Arcadians. *Personality:* simple, straightforward and rather unlucky. **Page 17.**

CALYPSO (cal-**ips**-oh) *Category:* demi-goddess; nymph. *Family Status:* d. of Atlas; lo. of Odysseus; possibly two/three s. (fa. Odysseus). *Career:* lived on island of Ortygia; fell in love with Odysseus when he called there on his travels; kept him with her by force for seven years; made to release him by Hermes on orders from Zeus. *Personality:* dominating; gets what she wants. *Supernatural Attributes:* long life; power to make mortals do what she wants. **Page 47.**

CASSANDRA (cass-**and**-ra) *Category:* mortal. *Family Status:* d. of King Priam and Queen Hecuba of Troy; slave and lo. of Agamemnon; twin s. (fa. Agamemnon). *Career:* Trojan princess; priestess of Apollo; seer; offended Apollo who cursed her never to be believed; tried to warn that Trojan War would bring disaster to Troy; taken prisoner by Agamemnon and returned to Mycenae with him; tried to warn him of Clytemnestra's murderous plans, but to no avail; slain by Clytemnestra. *Personality:* desperate and unhappy due to betraying Apollo; given to wailing and gnashing of teeth in despair. *Supernatural Attributes:* seeing future. *Associations:* someone (esp. female) who is always predicting bad news can be called a "Cassandra". **Page 41.**

CASTOR (**cass**-tor) *Category:* mortal. *Family Status:* twin s. of Tyndareus and Leda (his twin, Polydeuces, had Zeus as father, but the same mother and was born at the same time). *Career:* Argonaut; promising military skills, but killed young, along with his twin, in battle; went to Underworld as he was human, but Polydeuces went to Olympus as he was half-immortal; they could not bear separation and Polydeuces begged to go and join Castor in the Underworld; Zeus was touched and allowed them to spend alternate days in each place so they could be together. *Personality:* honourable, courageous; strong on family loyalty. *Distinguishing Features:* nearly always with his twin. *Associations:* sometimes called the Dioscuri; their image is set in the stars as Gemini, the twins.

CENTAURS (**sen**-tors) *Category:* demi-gods. *Family Status:* grands. of Ixion and Nephele. *Career:* usually employed as teachers of heroes; caused riot at a Lapith wedding. *Personalities:* wise, patient, brave but unreliable if given too much wine. *Distinguishing Features:* male human head and top half of body, bottom half of body and legs of a horse. *Supernatural Attributes:* unrivalled ability to teach riding, shooting bow and arrows and give advice at same time.

Centaur

Cerberus

CERBERUS (**sir**-ber-us) *Category:* monster. *Family Status:* child of Typhon and Echidne; Pluto's servant. *Career:* guarding gates of Underworld to prevent the dead leaving; was dragged to Earth to court of King Eurystheus as one of Twelve Labours of Heracles. *Personality:* ferocious; fond of snapping jaws and slaver-

ing; much to be feared on a trip to the Underworld. *Distinguishing Features:* he is a dog with three heads. *Supernatural Attributes:* immortality; his spittle produces aconite flowers, which contain the poison, wolf's bane. **Page 39.**

CERES (**seer**-eez) see **DEMETER.**

CERYNEAN HIND (**sair**-ee-nee-an) *Category:* animal; deer. *Family Status:* sacred to Artemis. *Career:* caught by Heracles as one of his Twelve Labours. *Personality:* shy; elusive. *Distinguishing Features:* golden horns. *Supernatural Attributes:* super-fast, almost impossible to catch. **Page 38.**

CHARON (**ka**-ron) *Category:* servant to the gods. *Career:* ferryman who rowed the dead across the River Styx into the Underworld; his fee was one obol (Ancient Greek coin). *Personality:* fierce, bad-tempered and menacing; miserly. *Distinguishing Features:* a white-haired old man with blazing eyes; often wore a hooded cloak. *Supernatural Attributes:* immortality; unavoidable on the journey to the Underworld. *Associations:* the Greeks always buried their dead with an obol in their mouth to pay Charon.

CHARYBDIS (kar-**rib**-diss) *Category:* natural phenomenon. *Family Status:* child of Typhon and Echidne. *Career:* wrecking ships and drowning humans; encountered by Odysseus, who managed to escape. *Personality:* pitiless; does not discriminate between good and evil. *Distinguishing Features:* it is a gigantic whirlpool; the monster, Scylla, is normally close by. **Page 47.**

CHIMAERA (kim-ear-a) *Category:* monster. *Career:* killing and devouring humans. *Personality:* extremely fierce; lethal to all ordinary mortals; killed by hero, Bellerophon, and winged horse, Pegasus. *Distinguishing Features:* head of a lion, body of a goat, serpent's tail. *Supernatural Attributes:* fire-breathing. *Associations:* a wildly improbably thing can be described as a "chimaera". **Page 28.**

Chimaera

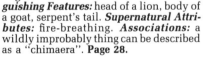

CIRCE (**sir**-see) *Category:* demi-goddess. *Family Status:* aunt of Medea; lo. of Odysseus; several s. (fa. Odysseus). *Career:* enchantress; practised magic on island of Aeaea; turned unwanted visitors into pigs; visited by Odysseus and used her spells on his men; impressed by Odysseus's courage and kept him as her lo. for a year; sent him to Underworld to consult Tiresias. *Personality:* lonely; wary; unreasonable to strangers. *Supernatural Attributes:* spell-casting. **Page 47.**

CLASHING ROCKS *Category:* natural phenomenon. *Career:* destroying sailors; positioned at entrance to Straits of Bosphorus; rocks clash shut if a ship tries to sail between them; attempted destruc-

tion of Jason and the Argonauts; also called Symplegades. *Personality:* impersonal will to destroy all mortals. *Distinguishing Features:* dark and menacing; craggy cliffs. *Supernatural Attributes:* opening and closing ability. **Page 32.**

CLYTEMNESTRA (kly-tem-**nest**-ra). *Category:* mortal. *Family Status:* d. of Tyndareus and Leda; m. Agamemnon against her will; one s. Orestes; three d. Iphigenia, Electra, Chrysothemis; m. Aegisthus. *Career:* Queen of Mycenae; became obsessed by hatred of Agamemnon; resulted in murder plot on his return from Trojan War; Aegisthus was her accomplice; killed in revenge by Orestes. *Personality:* embittered by experience; consumed with hatred of her husband. **Page 44.**

CREON (**kree**-on) *Category:* mortal. *Family Status:* brother of Jocasta; one s. Haemon; one d. Glauce. *Career:* King of Thebes after Oedipus; refused burial to Oedipus's son when he died in battle and threatened to punish Antigone when she found and buried him; killed in fire caused by Medea. *Personality:* strong and firm; somewhat unsympathetic. **Page 48.**

CRONOS (**kron**-oss) *Roman:* Saturn. *Category:* Titan. *Family Status:* s. of Uranus and Mother Earth; m. his sister, Titaness Rhea; three s. Poseidon, Pluto, Zeus; three d. Hera, Hestia, Demeter. *Career:* ruler of the world under Uranus; led rebellion against Uranus and became king of the gods; told he would be deposed by his own child so swallowed them all except the last one, Zeus, who was hidden from him; Zeus made him spew out his brothers and sisters then led a successful revolt against Cronos. *Personality:* mother-dominated; ruthless. *Distinguishing Features:* giant. *Supernatural Attributes:* immortality; gigantic strength. *Associations:* he is sometimes linked with Old Father Time with his scythe. **Page 8.**

CYCLOPES (**sye**-klo-peas) *Category:* demi-gods. *Family Status:* s. of Uranus and Mother Earth. *Career:* the original three were rejected and imprisoned in Tartarus by Uranus; rescued by Zeus; fought for Zeus against Titans; gave Zeus his thunderbolts, Pluto his helmet of invisibility and Poseidon his trident; killed by Apollo in revenge for death of Asclepius; their descendants lived on Sicily, working as shepherds or herdsmen; one of them, Polyphemus, imprisoned Odysseus when he visited. *Personality:* morose; bad-tempered. *Distinguishing Features:* giant size; one eye only in centre of forehead. *Supernatural Attributes:* extremely long life; enormous strength. **Pages 8, 46.**

Cyclops

DAEDALUS (**deed**-a-luss) *Category:* mortal. *Family Status:* one s. Icarus. *Career:* Athenian craftsman and inventor at court of King Minos; helped Minos's wife, Pasiphae, have love affair with a bull, resulting in birth of Minotaur; built Labyrinth to hold Minotaur; offended Minos, was imprisoned, but escaped by making wings of wax and feathers; passed linen thread through Triton shell by tying it to an ant. *Personality:* cunning; very clever with his hands; slippery customer. **Pages 26, 48.**

DANAE (**dan**-ee) *Category:* mortal. *Family Status:* d. of King Acrisius; lo. of Zeus; one s. Perseus. *Career:* princess; imprisoned by her father to prevent her marrying, as he was warned that he would be killed by his grandson; visited by Zeus as a shower of gold; gave birth to Perseus; set adrift in a boat with her son; Zeus guided them to Seriphos where King Polydictes looked after them; resisted advances of Polydictes for years; about to be forced to marry him when Perseus returned from adventures and turned him to stone, so she was free from his attentions. *Personality:* strong-willed. **Page 22.**

DANAUS (**dan-eh**-us) *Category:* mortal. *Family Status:* grands. of Poseidon; 50 d. *Career:* famous for inciting the mass-murder of his brother, Aegyptus's, 50 sons by his own daughters when they were forced to marry each other following a quarrel over their inheritance; daughters suitably punished in Tartarus. *Personality:* proud; unforgiving; careless of the penalties for killing relatives. **Page 25.**

DAPHNE (**daff**-nee) *Career:* demi-goddess; mountain-nymph. *Family Status:* d. of a river-god; refused to lo. of Apollo. *Career:* priestess of Mother Earth; defended her virtue by running away from Apollo; prayed to Mother Earth for help and was turned into a laurel tree; Apollo wore laurel wreath in her memory. *Personality:* pure; virtuous. *Distinguishing Features:* lived in mountains; fast runner. *Supernatural Attributes:* long life. **Page 16.**

DEIANEIRA (day-a-**neer**-a) *Category:* mortal. *Family Status:* second wife of Heracles. *Career:* almost carried off by the Centaur, Nessus, but saved by Heracles; caused the death of Heracles by being tricked into giving him a shirt which she believed contained a charm to keep him faithful to her; it was actually poisoned, caused agony and was impossible to remove so Heracles killed himself; she committed suicide. *Personality:* mistrustful; gullible. **Page 39.**

DEMETER (de-**meet**-a) *Roman:* Ceres. *Category:* goddess. *Family Status:* d. of Cronos and Rhea; two s. and two d. incl. Persephone (fa. Zeus). *Career:* goddess of the Earth and harvests; responsible for growth and fertility of fruit and crops; helped by Persephone; driven to desperation when Persephone seized by Pluto; abandoned her duties to search for her; after intervention by Zeus, had to accept a compromise – Persephone would spend half the year with her and half with Pluto; when Persephone is away, Demeter mourns and it is winter; accidentally ate shoulder of Pelops when served up to the gods for dinner by Tantalus. *Personality:*

strong maternal instinct, to the point of neglecting her duty; generous and bountiful. *Distinguishing Features:* often shown holding corn. *Supernatural Attributes:* immortality. **Page 11.**

DEUCALION (dew-**kale**-ee-on) *Category:* demi-god. *Family Status:* s. of Prometheus; m. Pyrrha; ancestor of whole human race. *Career:* warned by Prometheus when Zeus was about to flood the world and drown all mortals; survived by building a boat; when water subsided, obeyed the command of Zeus's messenger to throw stones over his shoulder – these became men; Pyrrha threw stones which became women, so human race began again. *Personality:* a good man; strong survival instinct. **Page 21.**

DIANA see **ARTEMIS.**

DIDO see **AENEAS.**

DIOMEDES (die-om-**ee**-deez) i. *Category:* mortal. *Career:* hero; fought for Greeks in Trojan War; wounded Aeneas; had the nerve to hurt Aphrodite when she came to Aeneas's rescue. *Personality:* daring – even foolhardy. **Page 42.**

DIOMEDES ii. *Category:* mortal. *Family Status:* s. of Ares and Cyrene. *Career:* king; owner of extremely vicious mares Heracles had to tame as one of his Twelve Labours; eaten by his horses. **Page 38.**

DIONYSUS (die-on-**eye**-sus) *Roman:* Bacchus. *Category:* god. *Family Status:* s. of Zeus and Semele; born from Zeus's thigh, where he was kept safe until his birth, after Semele was killed; m. Ariadne; six s. *Career:* god of wine and the theatre; travelled round teaching people how to make wine from grapes; led a life of pleasure; attracted fanatical followers, especially women, called Maenads; mystery cult formed to worship him; associated with drunkenness and licentious behaviour; deliberately provoked murder of Pentheus. *Personality:* fun-loving; womanizing; wild. *Distinguishing Features:* dark, curly hair, red lips, sparkling eyes; carries the thyrsos, a stick entwined with vine leaves; keeps undesirable company, such as Silenus and the satyrs. *Supernatural Attributes:* immortality; grants followers the power to tear animals (and people) limb from limb, bare-handed. **Pages 18, 19.**

DORUS (**door**-us) see **HELLEN.**

DRYADS (**dry**-adds) *Category:* demi-goddesses; tree-nymphs. *Personalities:* generally gentle and good. *Distinguishing Features:* beautiful; their life was linked to that of their tree. *Supernatural Attributes:* long life.

EAST WIND see **EURUS.**

ECHIDNE (ek-**kid**-nee) *Category:* monster. *Family Status:* six children, Orthrus (Geryon's dog), Cerberus, Hydra, Chimaera (fa. Typhon); Sphinx, Nemean Lion (fa. Orthrus). *Distinguishing Features:* half-woman, half-serpent. *Supernatural Attributes:* giving birth to monsters.

ECHO (**ekk**-o) *Category:* demi-goddess; nymph. *Family Status:* would-be lo. of Narcissus. *Career:* offended Hera and was condemned to repeat last few words that anyone said to her; fell in love with Narcissus but was rejected by him; pined away until only her voice was left. *Personality:* indiscreet; mournful and lonely. *Distinguishing Features:* unable to say anything of her own; invisible once she had faded away. *Supernatural Attributes:* long life. *Associations:* the way your words repeat if you shout them in the mountains or a tunnel is called an "echo". **Page 30.**

ELECTRA (ee-**lect**-ra) *Category:* mortal. *Family Status:* d. of Agamemnon and Clytemnestra; m. Pylades. *Career:* princess; badly affected by murder of her father by her mother; accessory to murder of her mother, by encouraging her brother, Orestes, to take revenge. *Personality:* vengeful; unforgiving. **Page 44.**

ENDYMION (en-**dim**-ee-on) *Category:* mortal. *Career:* fell in love with Selene; languished and dreamt about Selene; wished he need do nothing else; achieved a sort of immortality when his wish was granted by Zeus and he put him into eternal sleep in which he never grew old. *Personality:* romantic, dreamy. *Distinguishing Features:* in permanent sleep. *Supernatural Attributes:* eternally young. **Page 17.**

EOS (**ee**-oss) *Roman:* Aurora. *Category:* goddess. *Family Status:* d. of Hyperion and the Titaness, Theia; lo. of Orion. *Career:* goddess of the dawn; responsible for the rising of the sun each morning; drove a chariot; cursed by Aphrodite to fall for lots of young men, after she had an affair with Ares; was slighted by Orion, who abandoned her to go hunting with Artemis. *Personality:* fond of men. *Distinguishing Features:* thought of as coloured liked the dawn sky – rosy-fingered, saffron-robed. *Supernatural Attributes:* immortality. **Page 29.**

EPIMETHEUS (epp-ee-**mee**-thyoos) *Category:* Titan. *Family Status:* brother to Prometheus; one d. Pyrrha. *Career:* rather ineffectually helped his brother with the creation of mankind; he welcomed Pandora, though he had been warned not to accept gifts from Zeus, and thereby hastened the introduction of evil into the world by Pandora's curiosity; his name means "afterthought." *Personality:* easily taken in; susceptible to a pretty girl. *Supernatural Attributes:* immortality. **Page 21.**

ERINYES (air-**in**-yeez) *Category:* demi-goddesses. *Family Status:* sprang from Uranus's blood. *Career:* appointed by the gods to trouble the conscience of murderers, especially those who murder rela-

Erinye

tives. **Personalities:** persistent; terrifying to the guilty – no trouble at all to the innocent. **Distinguishing Features:** three of them; normally considered to be female; when in pursuit, they have a dog's head, snakes for hair and bats' wings. **Supernatural Attributes:** immortality; ability to inflict mental torture on victims. **Associations:** euphemistically called Eumenides (Kindly Ones). **Pages 8, 45.**

ERIS (**air**-iss) **Category:** goddess. **Family Status:** d. of Zeus and Hera; twin to Ares. **Career:** goddess of spite; cause of the Trojan War by bringing golden apple inscribed "For the fairest" to wedding feast of Thetis and Peleus. **Personality:** spiteful; trouble-making; revengeful. **Supernatural Attributes:** immortality.

EROS (**ear**-oss) **Roman:** Cupid. **Category:** god. **Family Status:** not clear; sometimes said to be s. of Ares and Aphrodite; m. Psyche. **Career:** specialized in making people fall in love – even unsuitable couples;  Eros
fell in love with Psyche when grazed with his own arrow; became her lo. in secret; when the secret was disclosed, Aphrodite was furious and Eros was forbidden to see Psyche; Zeus was touched by Eros and Psyche's joint efforts to gain the forgiveness of Aphrodite and made Psyche immortal so they could marry and live together on Olympus. **Personality:** mischievous; fond of romantic intrigues. **Distinguishing Features:** young and handsome; charming; carried gold bow and arrows, used to make people fall in love; has wings. **Supernatural Attributes:** immortality; irresistible love-inducing ability. **Pages 13, 31.**

EUMENIDES (you-**men**-ee-deez) see **ERINYES.**

EURIPIDES (you-**rip**-ee-deez) Real person, who wrote plays using stories from myths. Lived from 480-406 BC.

EUROPA (you-**rope**-a) **Category:** mortal. **Family Status:** sister of Cadmus; lo. of Zeus; three s. Minos, Rhadamanthys, Sarpedon (fa. Zeus); m. King of Crete. **Career:** carefree childhood until carried off by Zeus in the form of a white bull; taken to Crete, where she had his three sons; later m. the king and got him to accept Minos as heir to the throne. **Personality:** naive, loving. **Page 22.**

EURUS (**your**-us) **Category:** god. **Family Status:** kept by Aeolus in a bag. **Career:** East Wind; blew as the gods directed. **Personality:** violent and disorderly. **Distinguishing Features:** sometimes given a serpent's tail. **Supernatural Attributes:** immortality; creating storms.

EURYDICE (you-**rid**-ee-see) **Category:** demi-goddess; dryad. **Family Status:** m. Orpheus. **Career:** happy as Orpheus's wife until bothered by the attentions of

Aristaeus; running from him, she received a lethal snake-bite; Orpheus followed her to the Underworld to beg Pluto to let her go; he succeeded, but broke conditions of her release by turning to look at her before she had left the gates of the Underworld; they were re-united after Orpheus's death. **Personality:** faithful, sad. **Page 31.**

EURYSTHEUS (you-**riss**-thyoos) **Category:** mortal. **Career:** king; chosen by the Oracle as the man to set the Twelve Labours for Heracles; he suffered the consequences, as Heracles brought terrifying live trophies to show him. **Personality:** rather cowardly; not a man of action. **Page 37.**

FURIES (**fyoor**-eez) see **ERINYES.**

GALATEA (gal-at-**tay**-a) **Category:** became mortal. **Family Status:** m. Pygmalion. **Career:** was created as a statue by Pygmalion; he fell in love with her; Aphrodite was moved by his love for her and brought her to life; they lived happily ever after. **Personality:** loving and dutiful. **Distinguishing Features:** statuesque. **Page 13.**

GANYMEDE (**gan**-ee-meed) **Category:** mortal, becoming immortal. **Family Status:** s. of King Tros; loved by Eos and Zeus. **Career:** was snatched up to Olympus by an eagle sent by Zeus; took over from Hebe as cup-bearer to the gods. **Personality:** attractive; athletic. **Distinguishing Features:** extremely handsome. **Supernatural Attributes:** immortality, once he was taken to Olympus. **Associations:** his image set in the stars as Aquarius, the water-carrier. **Page 48.**

GERYON (gair-**eye**-on) **Category:** giant. **Career:** owner and guardian of marvellous cattle; killed by Heracles, who had to capture the cattle for one of his Twelve Labours. **Personality:** aggressive in defence of his property. **Distinguishing Features:** three bodies above the waist. **Supernatural Attributes:** enormous size; triple weapon-wielding ability. **Page 38.**

GLAUCIS (**glaw**-sis) **Category:** mortal. **Family Status:** was to m. Jason. **Career:** innocently intending to become Jason's wife, when she suffered a horrible death; on the eve of the wedding, Medea gave her a dress and crown as presents, which burst into flames when she put them on. **Personality:** blameless victim. **Page 33.**

GLAUCUS (**glaw**-kuss) **Category:** mortal. **Family Status:** one s. Bellerophon. **Career:** king; offended Aphrodite, who fed his horses magic herbs and water from her well on the eve of a chariot race so they bolted and killed him. **Personality:** rather reckless. **Page 13.**

GOLDEN RACE: Category: mortal. **Family Status:** created by Zeus; no children. **Career:** created to live on Earth; blissful existence in peaceful world; shortlived, as the whole race died out through not having children; their spirits lingered on in tranquil places and helped and protected later races. **Personality:** good, peaceable, beneficient. **Super-**

natural Attributes: their protective spirits can be sensed by humans. **Page 20.**

GORGONS (**gore**-gonz) **Category:** monsters. **Family Status:** three d. of Phorcys — two immortal, one mortal. **Career:** once beautiful, were turned into hideous monsters for offending Athene; turned anyone who looked at them to stone; one of them,  Gorgon
Medusa, was killed by Perseus. **Personalities:** evil, destructive. **Distinguishing Features:** wings, bronze claws, serpents for hair; their lair could be easily recognized by worn statues of victims. **Supernatural Attributes:** turning people to stone. **Page 24.**

HADES (**hay**-deez) Another name for Pluto, god of the Underworld, or for the Underworld itself. See **PLUTO.**

HAEMON (**he**-mon) **Category:** mortal. **Family Status:** s. of Creon; lo. of Antigone. **Career:** prince; Antigone hanged herself after his father condemned her to death for finding and burying her brother who was killed in battle; killed himself. **Personality:** brave and defiant. **Page 48.**

HARMONIA (har-**moan**-ee-a) **Category:** goddess. **Family Status:** d. of Aphrodite and Ares; m. Cadmus. **Career:** bringing back peace after war to prepare the way for her mother, the goddess of love, to return; went to Isles of the Blessed when she died. **Personality:** diplomatic, tactful. **Supernatural Attributes:** immortality. **Page 13.**

HARPIES (**har**-peez) **Category:** monsters. **Career:** taking victims to Erinyes for punishment; pestering human victims by stealing their food and screeching so they cannot sleep; harried King Phineas until  Harpy
driven from his court by Jason and the Argonauts. **Personality:** nasty; persistent and tireless; extremely unwelcome visitors. **Distinguishing Features:** birds with nagging, female heads. **Supernatural Attributes:** flying and nagging abilities in deadly combination. **Page 32.**

HEBE (**hee**-bee) **Category:** goddess. **Family Status:** d. of Zeus and Hera; sometimes said to have married Heracles when he became immortal. **Career:** cup-bearer to the gods; made redundant by Ganymede who took the job when brought to Olympus by Zeus. **Personality:** obliging and helpful. **Distinguishing Features:** often carries a jug of nectar. **Supernatural Attributes:** immortality. **Page 48.**

HECTOR (**heck**-tor) **Category:** mortal. **Family Status:** s. of King Priam and Queen Hecuba of Troy; m. Andromache. **Career:** professional warrior; great hero for Troy in Trojan War; killed Patroclus; humiliated in death when killed by furious Achilles and dragged round the walls of Troy behind his chariot; Trojans had to pay to get his body for burial. **Personality:** noble and brave; good leader. **Page 42.**

HECUBA (**heck**-you-ba) **Category:** mortal. **Family Status:** m. King Priam of Troy; children incl. Hector, Paris, Cassandra. **Career:** queen. **Page 40.**

HELEN (**hell**-en) **Category:** demi-goddess. **Family Status:** d. of Zeus and Leda; m. Menelaus; one d. Hermione; lo. of Paris. **Career:** abducted by Theseus as a child but rescued by her brothers, Castor and Polydeuces; obediently married according to her step-father, Tyndareus's, wishes; caught up in divine plotting when Aphrodite promised Paris would have her in return for choosing herself as the loveliest goddess; she fell in love with Paris and ran away with him, which started the Trojan War; surprisingly, she was taken back by Menelaus at the end of the war; taken to Olympus by Zeus; became goddess of sailors. **Personality:** much desired by men; she sometimes hated herself for the trouble her beauty caused. **Distinguishing Features:** the most beautiful woman in the world. **Associations:** hers was "the face which launched a thousand ships" (meaning the fleet that sailed to Troy), in "Doctor Faustus" by Christopher Marlowe. **Page 41.**

HELIOS (**hee**-lee-oss) **Category:** Titan. **Family Status:** descended from Uranus and Mother Earth; one s. Phaeton. **Career:** keeper of sacred cattle; drove chariot of the sun across the sky each day; foolishly allowed Phaeton to have a go at the reins; Phaeton's reckless driving endangered the Earth and he was killed by Zeus. **Personality:** over-indulgent father. **Distinguishing Features:** golden, shining, like the sun. **Supernatural Attributes:** immortality. **Associations:** his name has been used for things associated with the sun e.g. the flower, heliotrope, which turns to follow the sun and the gas, Helium, first discovered among gases surrounding the sun. **Page 26.**

HELLE (**hell**-a) **Category:** mortal. **Family Status:** d. of Athamas and Nephele, the cloud-woman. **Career:** unreasonably hated by her step-mother, Ino; escaped with her brother, Phrixus, on back of golden ram sent by Hera; she fell from the ram's back into the sea as it crossed from Europe to Asia. **Personality:** innocent victim. **Associations:** the strip of water where Europe (Greece) meets Asia (Turkey) was named the Hellespont (Sea of Helle) after her. **Page 25.**

HELLEN (**hell**-en) **Category:** demi-god. **Family Status:** s. of Deucalion; grands. of Prometheus; s. incl. Aeolus, Dorus; grands. include Ion, Achaeus. **Career:** legendary founder of four so-called Hellenic races – Aeolians, Dorians, Ionians and Achaeans. **Personality:** noble; dynasty-building. **Associations:** the Greeks still call their country Hellas. **Page 48.**

HEPHAESTOS (heff-**eest**-oss) **Roman:** Vulcan. **Category:** god. **Family Status:** s. of Hera alone; m. Aphrodite. **Career:** rather hard-done-by; born lame; thrown from Olympus in a rage by Hera and crippled; m. Aphrodite at Zeus's command, against her will – suffered her infidelities; employed as smith in the gods' forge; skilled craftsman, called upon to make armour and jewels for the gods; respected and admired for his work in the end. **Personality:** tends to keep in the background; even-tempered except when especially roused to jealousy by Aphrodite; hard-working; good with his hands; beneficient, kindly; **Distinguishing Features:** strong but coarse; dark, deformed; usually to be found in his forge, with tools of his trade. **Supernatural Attributes:** immortality; crafting super-protective weapons for special purposes. **Page 12.**

HERA (**hair**-a) **Roman:** Juno. **Category:** goddess. **Family Status:** d. of Cronos and Rhea; m. her brother, Zeus; two s. Ares (fa. Zeus), Hephaestos (no father); two d. Eris, Hebe (fa. Zeus). **Career:** Queen of the gods and protectress of women but spent a lot of time pursuing Zeus's lovers and devising punishments for them; rivalry between herself, Athene and Aphrodite; supported Greeks in Trojan War because she held a grudge against Paris, for choosing Aphrodite as the most beautiful goddess; little evidence of any kindly feelings towards mortals; especially made Heracles's life a misery. **Personality:** haughty; jealous; vain; sometimes cruel. **Distinguishing Features:** one of the most beautiful goddesses; famed for her white arms – a sign of beauty. **Supernatural Attributes:** immortality; can inflict madness. **Associations:** the peacock was her symbol – she set the eyes of her 100-eyed servant, Argus, in its tail. **Pages 9, 11.**

HERACLES (**hair**-a-kleez) **Roman:** Hercules. **Category:** demi-god. **Family Status:** s. of Zeus and Alcmene; m. Megara; m. Deianeira; several children with both wives; sometimes said to have married Hebe when made immortal. **Career:** adventuring; Argonaut; fighting monsters; unfairly hounded by Hera, who was jealous of Zeus's affair with his mother; was driven temporarily mad by Hera and killed his first wife and children; although it was not his fault, he had to make amends for their deaths; consulted the Oracle and was told to perform Twelve Labours (impossible tasks) set by King Eurystheus; managed them all successfully – mostly feats of strength; purged his guilt and he re-married; premature death when tricked into wearing a poisoned shirt given to him innocently by Deianeira; he could not take it off, nor bear the pain, so he built a pyre and climbed on it to die; Zeus rescued him and took him to Olympus to be an Immortal; left his bow to Philoctetes. **Personality:** exceptionally strong and brave; man of action, not thought. **Distinguishing Features:** hugely-built and powerful; wore extra-tough skin from Nemean lion as a cape for protection. **Supernatural Attributes:** super-human strength; immortality, once taken to Olympus by Zeus. **Pages 37, 38, 39.**

HERMES (**her**-meez) **Roman:** Mercury. **Category:** god. **Family Status:** s. of Zeus and Titaness Maia. **Career:** precocious and naughty as a child; stole Apollo's cattle; won Apollo's forgiveness by inventing lyre and giving it to him; given job as messenger of the gods, carrying Zeus's commands, to keep him out of trouble; was also the god of thieves because of stealing Apollo's cattle and of treaties because of his diplomatic way of calming Apollo; said to have invented the alphabet, boxing and gymnastics. **Personality:** quick-witted; energetic; somewhat mischievous, even a thief; excellent at bargaining to his own advantage; inventive. **Distinguishing Features:** winged helmet and sandals. **Supernatural Attributes:** speedy flight for delivering messages; immortality. **Associations:** Roman name given to the substance Mercury because it moves so quickly when in liquid metal form. **Page 19.**

Hermes

HERMIONE (her-**my**-on-nee) **Category:** mortal. **Family Status:** d. of Menelaus and Helen; m. Orestes.

HESIONE (hess-**eye**-on-ee) see **PRIAM.**

HESPERIDES (hess-**pair**-ee-deez) **Category:** demi-goddesses. **Family Status:** d. of Atlas and Hesperis. **Career:** gardeners; looked after Hera's golden apples of immortality; allowed Atlas to take some to give to Heracles for one of his Twelve Labours; sweet singers. **Personalities:** patient; kindly. **Supernatural Attributes:** immortality. **Page 39.**

HESTIA (**hess**-tee-a) **Roman:** Vesta. **Category:** goddess. **Family Status:** d. of Cronos and Rhea. **Career:** protectress of the hearth; she was very popular – protected homes and was well-loved; did not get involved much in adventures and fights; gave up her place on Olympus to Dionysus. **Personality:** protective; gentle; kind. **Distinguishing Features:** virgin goddess. **Supernatural Attributes:** immortality; powerful protecting ability.

HIPPODAMIA (hip-o-dam-**me**-a) **Category:** mortal. **Family Status:** d. of King Oenomaus; m. Pelops; many children incl. Atreus. **Career:** princess; swept off her feet by Pelops and married him, although he killed her father in a chariot race; **Personality:** romantically reckless. **Page 49.**

HIPPOLYTE (hip-**pol**-ee-tee) **Category:** mortal. **Family Status:** m. Theseus; one s. Hippolytus. **Career:** warrior Queen of the Amazons; would have given her girdle (belt) freely to Heracles when he had to fetch it as one of his Twelve Labours, but Hera caused the Amazons to attack him so he had to fight for it; fought at Theseus's side and died in battle. **Personality:** fierce, **Distinguishing Features:** tall and strong; favoured warrior dress. **Pages 36, 38.**

HIPPOLYTUS (hip-**poll**-it-us) **Category:**

mortal. *Family Status:* s. of Theseus and Hippolyte. *Career:* unfortunate victim of his stepmother, Phaedra; she claimed he had attacked her; Theseus prayed to Poseidon to punish his son; Poseidon sent a great wave to kill him, although he was innocent. *Personality:* honourable; honest. **Page 25.**

HOMER (**home**-er) Real man. Supposed author of The Iliad, The Odyssey.

HYACINTHUS (hi-a-**sinth**-us) *Category:* mortal. *Career:* Spartan prince; he was favoured by the gods and became special friend of Apollo; the West Wind was jealous and plotted his downfall – blew a discus thrown by Hyacinthus back in his face and killed him. *Personality:* carefree; pleasure-seeking. *Distinguishing Features:* very handsome; athletic. *Associations:* where his blood fell the first hyacinth flowers grew. **Page 48.**

Hyacinth

HYPERION (hi-**peer**-ee-on) *Category:* Titan. *Family Status:* s. of Uranus and Mother Earth; one s. Helios; two d. Eos (the dawn) and Selene (the moon). *Career:* sun-god – eclipsed by Apollo when New Gods took over from Titans. *Distinguishing Features:* bright, shining, golden. *Supernatural Attributes:* immortality.

ICARUS (**ick**-er-us) *Category:* mortal. *Family Status:* s. of Daedalus. *Career:* high-flying but brief; imprisoned with his father when Daedalus displeased Minos; escaped on wings of wax and feathers made by Daedalus; got carried away by being able to fly, went too close to the sun which melted the wax and the wings disintegrated; fell into the sea and was killed. *Personality:* arrogant, ambitious. *Associations:* the sea where he fell to his death is called Icarian after him. **Page 26.**

INO (**ee**-no) *Category:* mortal. *Family Status:* d. of Cadmus; m. Athamas; two s. *Career:* desperate for her own son to be heir to the throne, she wanted to dispose of her step-children, Phrixus and Helle; hatched devious plan to make Athamas think he must sacrifice his son; foiled by Hera, who got Hermes to send golden ram to rescue the children. *Personality:* many unpleasant characteristics – jealous, selfish, cruel and cunning. **Page 25.**

IO (**ee**-oh) *Category:* mortal. *Family Status:* d. of river-god, Inachus; lo. of Zeus. *Career:* priestess of Hera; attracted Zeus's attention and he turned her into a cow to keep the affair from Hera; Hera tied the cow up and placed Argus to guard her; Hermes released her but Hera sent a gadfly to sting her non-stop; she ran to Egypt where she became a woman again and a priestess of the Egyptian goddess, Isis. *Personality:* mild, loving. *Distinguishing Features:* beautiful; took the form of a gentle white cow during her transformation. **Page 22.**

ION (**ee**-on) see **HELLEN.**

IPHIGENIA (if-ij-a-**nee**-a) *Category:* mortal. *Family Status:* d. of Agamemnon and Clytemnestra. *Career:* on the point of being sacrificed by her father to gain a good wind to sail to Troy, was saved by Artemis, who put a deer in her place; assumed dead, but actually became priestess of Artemis among the Taurians; she rescued her brother, Orestes, when he was about to be sacrificed by the Taurians for stealing their statue of Artemis; never married. *Personality:* rather serious; dedicated priestess. **Page 17.**

IRIS (**eye**-riss) *Category:* goddess. *Career:* goddess of the rainbow and messenger of Hera. *Personality:* obedient; quiet *Supernatural Attributes:* immortality.

IXION (**icks**-ee-on) *Category:* mortal. *Career:* King of the Lapiths; nasty piece of work; murdered his future father-in-law; planned to steal Hera from Zeus; Zeus made Nephele out of clouds as Hera's double, to test Ixion; he fell for the trick and attempted to grab her; his guilt was thus proved and Zeus had him tied to a wheel of fire which was sent rolling across the heavens fogever. *Personality:* arrogant, presumptuous; defiant of the gods. **Page 26.**

JASON (**jace**-on) *Category:* mortal. *Family Status:* nephew of Pelias. *Career:* cheated of his inheritance to the throne of Iolcus by Pelias; grew up in exile; returned to claim his throne – was told he could be heir if he brought golden fleece from Colchis; set out in a ship (Argo), with many heroes (Argonauts); had many adventures; was helped by Medea to steal the fleece from its dragon-serpent guard; returned to Iolcus with Medea; she caused death of Pelias so the people banished her and Jason; he became King of Corinth; decided to abandon Medea to marry Princess Glauce; Medea caused Glauce's death and the Corinthians banished them too; ended his life as an outcast; was sitting under the rotting remains of the Argo when prow fell and killed him. *Personality:* heroic, ambitious; became too proud and greedy for power; hurt those who loved him. *Supernatural Attributes:* had special help from the gods (Hera and Aphrodite made Medea fall in love with him and help him) before he lost their favour by his behaviour. **Pages 32, 33.**

JOCASTA (jock-**ass**-ta) *Category:* mortal. *Family Status:* m. Laius; one s. Oedipus; m. Oedipus; two s. and two d. (fa. Oedipus). *Career:* Queen of Thebes; destined for a terrible Fate; was told by Oracle that her son would murder his father and marry his mother, so abandoned Oedipus to die; he survived, unknowingly killed his father in a roadside dispute and later came to Thebes as a hero for killing the Sphinx; his reward was to marry Jocasta and become king; this fulfilled the prophesy; when the truth was revealed, she hanged herself in shame. *Personality:* high-principled; respectful; good. **Page 29.**

LAIUS (**lay**-us) *Category:* mortal. *Family Status:* m. Jocasta; one s. Oedipus. *Career:* King of Thebes; fell foul of Oracle which predicted he would be killed by his own son; despite efforts to avoid it by exposing Oedipus to die, the baby survived and Laius met him (without recognizing him) when he grew up and quarrelled with him over who should give way on a road; they fought and Oedipus killed him, so the prophecy came true. See also **JOCASTA** and **OEDIPUS.** *Personality:* stubborn, unlucky. **Page 29.**

LEDA (**leed**-a) *Category:* mortal. *Family Status:* m. King Tyndareus of Sparta; lo. of Zeus; two s. Castor (fa. Tyndareus), Polydeuces (fa. Zeus); two d. Clytemnestra (fa. Tyndareus), Helen (fa. Zeus). *Career:* Queen of Sparta; seduced by Zeus disguised as a swan – their daughter, Helen, was the most beautiful woman in the world and the outward cause of the Trojan War. *Personality:* straightforward, good. *Distinguishing Features:* beautiful enough to catch Zeus's eye. **Page 23.**

LERNEAN HYDRA (lern-**ee**-an **hi**-dra) *Category:* monster. *Career:* death and destruction; terrorized swamps of Lerna; killed by Heracles as one of his Twelve Labours. *Personality:* vicious; not keen on humans. *Distinguishing Features:* dog-like body; many serpent's heads. *Supernatural Attributes:* heads grow again when cut off – this can only be prevented by sealing the severed neck with fire. **Page 37.**

Hydra

LETO (**lee**-toe) *Category:* Titaness. *Family Status:* lo. of Zeus; one s. Apollo (fa. Zeus); one d. Artemis (fa. Zeus). *Career:* had affair with Zeus; was persecuted by Hera, who set her giant snake, Python, on Leto out of jealousy; the South Wind helped by carrying her to Ortygia, where Artemis was born; Artemis helped her to Delos, where Apollo was born; rewarded by the fierce protection of her twin children. *Personality:* brave, long-suffering. *Supernatural Attributes:* immortality. *Associations:* quail was her bird. **Page 16.**

LOTUS-EATERS (**low**-tuss eaters) *Category:* mortals. *Career:* eating lotus-fruit; these caused people to forget everything except wanting to eat more of the flowers. *Personalities:* robbed of personality by poisonous effect of the flowers, which erased all memories. *Distinguishing Features:* only to be found in Libya, where lotus-flowers grew; permanently in a dream-like trance. **Page 46.**

Lotus

MAENADS (**meen**-adds) *Roman:* Bacchantes. *Category:* mortals. *Career:*

women followers of Dionysus; infamous for frenzied behaviour and wild dancing during their ceremonies. See **AGAVE, PENTHEUS**. *Personalities:* normal, until under the influence of Dionysian rites, when they could become violent if disturbed. *Distinguishing Features:* female; wear fawn-skins; carry thyrsos, stick wrapped with ivy. *Supernatural Attributes:* superhuman strength when in religious trance – could tear animals to pieces with their bare hands. **Page 19.**

MAIA (my-a) *Category:* Titaness. *Family Status:* d. of Atlas; lo. of Zeus; one s. Hermes (fa. Zeus). *Career:* surprisingly peaceful, unlike most of Zeus's lovers. *Supernatural Attributes:* immortality.

MARSYAS (mar-see-ass) *Category:* demigod; satyr. *Career:* usual satyr-like preoccupations – chasing nymphs, getting drunk with Dionysus, enjoying himself; found the cursed flute Athene threw away; foolishly challenged Apollo to a music contest in which the loser was to be killed; he lost and Apollo skinned him alive. *Personality:* pleasure-seeking; womanizing; lack of respect for the gods. *Distinguishing Features:* horse's ears and tail. **Page 16.**

MEDEA (med-**dee**-a) *Category:* mortal. *Family Status:* d. of King Aeetes; lo. of Jason; m. Aegeus; one s. . *Career:* professional enchantress; fell in love with Jason when he came to seek the golden fleece; betrayed her father to help him, then escaped with him; killed her half-brother; tricked Pelias's daughters into killing Pelias; caused herself and Jason to be banished from Iolcus; was heiress to throne of Corinth, so went there and made Jason king; furious when Jason decided to marry Princess Glauce – sent her a poisoned dress and crown as "gifts", which killed her when she put them on; fled from Corinth; sometimes accused of killing her children first, though it may have been the Corinthians who did it; tried to poison Theseus while m. to Aegeus; cured Heracles of his madness; she became an Immortal and ruled the Elysian Fields; some say she m. Achilles in the Underworld. *Personality:* extreme; passionate. *Distinguishing Features:* drove a chariot pulled by dragon-serpents. *Supernatural Attributes:* skilled in making magic potions. **Pages 32, 33.**

MEDUSA (med-**yoos**-a) *Category:* monster; Gorgon. *Family Status:* d. of sea-god, Phorcys; Pegasus sprang from her blood. *Career:* she offended Athene, who turned her and her sisters into monsters; from then on, turning humans to stone became her main pastime; was killed by Perseus, with the help of weapons from the gods. *Personality:* vindictive; impersonal hatred of all humans. *Distinguishing Features:* protruding tongue, bulging eyes, serpents instead of hair, wings, bronze claws; her home can be recognized by crumbling statues of humans surrounding it. *Supernatural Attributes:* able to petrify people. **Page 24.**

MEGARA (meg-er-a) see **HERACLES**.

MENELAUS (men-a-**lay**-us) *Category:* mortal. *Family Status:* brother of Agamemnon; m. Helen; one d. Hermione. *Career:* King of Sparta; chosen as Helen's husband from all the Greek princes; sadly, she did not love him; when she was abducted by Paris, Menelaus and Agamemnon raised a force against Troy and embarked on the Trojan War; after the war, he found he still loved Helen and took her back. *Personality:* rough and ready; brave but not too bright. *Distinguishing Features:* good at making loud war-cry. **Pages 41, 43.**

METIS (meet-iss) *Category:* Titaness. *Family Status:* lo. of Zeus. *Career:* Titaness of wisdom; advised Zeus; she was expecting Zeus's child when it was predicted that if she had a son, he would be greater than his father, so Zeus turned her into a fly and swallowed her; he later developed a headache, had his skull broken open and out came Athene. *Personality:* very clever and wise. *Supernatural Attributes:* her wisdom lived on through Athene. **Page 14.**

MIDAS (my-dass) *Category:* mortal. *Family Status:* one d. *Career:* helped Silenus when drunk and earned reward from Dionysus; wished that everything he touched should turn to gold; soon his palace, his food and even his d. had turned to gold and he was starving and lonely; the wish was undone; offended Apollo and was given ass's ears as punishment; hid them under his cap, but his barber saw them and word got out that Midas had been punished for his foolishness. *Personality:* thoughtless; greedy for riches; rather stupid; obstinate. *Supernatural Attributes:* ability to turn things to gold during the time Dionysus granted his wish. **Page 27.**

MINERVA (min-**urv**-a) see **ATHENE**.

MINOS (my-noss) *Category:* mortal. *Family Status:* s. of Zeus and Europa; m. Pasiphae; one s. Androgeus; two d. Ariadne, Phaedra. *Career:* powerful king of Crete; successful warrior – defeated Nisus with the help of his treacherous daughter, Scylla; guardian of the Minotaur; demanded hostages from the mainland to feed to the Minotaur in compensation for the death of his son, whom the Greeks had killed; betrayed by Ariadne when she helped Theseus kill the Minotaur, then escaped with him; became a judge of the dead when he died. *Personality:* strong but harsh and not well-loved by his daughter or wife. **Pages 34, 36, 48.**

MINOTAUR (my-no-tore) *Category:* monster. *Family Status:* s. of Poseidon's bull and Pasiphae. *Career:* lived in Labyrinth designed by Daedalus; ate human flesh; killed by Theseus. *Personality:* evil, murderous, full of hatred. *Distinguishing Features:* head and shoulders of a bull, body of a man. *Supernatural Attributes:* fantastic strength and devouring ability. **Pages 34, 36.**

Minotaur

MOPSUS (mop-suss) *Category:* prophet. *Career:* renowned seer; official advisor to the Argonauts. *Supernatural Attributes:* seeing the future.

MOTHER EARTH *Category:* goddess. *Family Status:* emerged into existence from Chaos; one s. Uranus; m. Uranus; many children – plants and animals, the Cyclopes, strange-shaped giants and monsters, the Titans. *Career:* creating the Earth and giving birth to creatures that populate it; developed hatred for Uranus and successfully encouraged her son, Cronos, to rebel against him; answered Daphne's prayer when she was fleeing from Apollo, by turning her into a laurel tree; angered by Orion saying he could kill all monsters, as they were all her children. *Personality:* motherly; protective; gets angry if her children are mistreated. *Distinguishing Features:* she is the Earth. *Supernatural Attributes:* giving birth to supernatural beings; immortality. *Associations:* also called Ge or Gaia. **Pages 8, 29.**

MUSES (myooz-iz) *Category:* demigoddesses. *Family Status:* nine d. of Zeus and Mnemosyne (memory). *Career:* inspiring creativity in artists and scientists; originally lived wild on Mount Parnassus but were tamed by Apollo and became his companions. *Personalities:* creative; artistic; elusive. *Distinguishing Features:* beautiful young women. *Supernatural Attributes:* immortality; able to inspire intellectual endeavour. **Page 16.**

MYRTILUS (mer-**till**-uss) *Category:* mortal. *Career:* charioteer to King Oenomaus; sabotaged the king's chariot before the race with Pelops, so it crashed, Oenomaus was killed and Pelops could marry his daughter, Hippodamia; his thanks from Pelops was to be thrown out of his chariot while they were escaping; he drowned. *Personality:* not to be trusted; disloyal; selfish. *Associations:* linked with myrtle, Aphrodite's flower. **Page 49.**

NAIADS (nye-adds) *Category:* demigoddesses. *Career:* they were spirits of nature who lived in streams and waterfalls; often attended a god or goddess; could harm mortals but did not often do so. *Personalities:* generally happy and kind. *Distinguishing Features:* pretty young maidens; to be found near fresh water sources. *Supernatural Attributes:* long life.

NARCISSUS (nar-**sis**-us) *Category:* mortal. *Career:* concern for his own beauty; hurting anyone who fell in love with him by his indifference and egotism; caused Echo to fade away to nothing for unrequited love; punished by Artemis, who made him fall in love with his own reflection; committed suicide when he realized he would never love anyone better than himself. *Personality:* exceedingly vain; callous; insensi-

Narcissus

tive to others. *Distinguishing Features:* excessive good looks. *Associations:* gave his name to flower, narcissus; self-love can be called "narcissism". **Page 30.**

NEMESIS (nem-a-sis) *Category:* goddess. *Career:* she brought retribution (just punishment) to people who did wrong; especially punished presumptuousness towards the gods. *Personality:* remorseless; unavoidable. *Supernatural Attributes:* immortality.

NEOPTOLEMUS (nee-op-**tol**-ee-muss) *Roman:* Pyrrhus. *Career:* mortal. *Family Status:* s. of Achilles and Deidamia. *Career:* miltary; fought by his father at Troy; inherited Achilles's armour after Ajax and Agamemnon argued over it; entered Troy inside the Wooden Horse; killed Hector's son and carried off Andromache. *Personality:* daring; vengeful; arrogant. **Page 42.**

NEPHELE (neff-ee-lee) *Category:* demi-goddess. *Family Status:* created by Zeus out of clouds; m. Athamas; two s. incl. Phrixus; one d. Helle. *Career:* rather unhappy; made by Zeus to test Ixion – he tried to seize her, proving his wickedness; put aside by Athamas for new wife, Ino; had reason to be much concerned about her children under Ino's care; prayed to Hera to protect them and she answered by sending golden ram to rescue them. *Personality:* insubstantial character; mistreated; fond mother. *Distinguishing Features:* made of clouds in the image of Hera. *Supernatural Attributes:* cannot be caught and held by a mortal because has no solid shape. **Page 26.**

NEREIDS (near-eh-ids) *Category:* demi-goddesses. *Family Status:* d. of Nereus and Doris, sea-deities. *Career:* attending on sea-gods; sometimes involved in mortal lives. *Personalities:* proud, independent. *Distinguishing Features:* their natural form was as beautiful women. *Supernatural Attributes:* could change shape at will, like most sea-deities. See **THETIS. Pages 23, 24.**

NEW GODS The New Gods were **ZEUS, POSEIDON, PLUTO, HESTIA, HERA, DEMETER.**

NIOBE (nye-oh-bee) *Category:* mortal. *Family Status:* sister of Pelops; seven s.; seven d. *Career:* Queen of Thebes; condemned herself when she boasted she was better than Leto as she had seven sons and daughters while Leto had only one of each (Apollo and Artemis); Apollo and Artemis killed all her children except one s. and one d.; she grieved so severely that Zeus took pity and turned her to stone at the peak of Mount Sipylus to stop her suffering. *Personality:* excessive pride in her family leading to boastfulness; foolish lack of respect for the gods; very sad, after the loss of her children. *Distinguishing Features:* turned to stone by Zeus. *Associations:* each year when the snow melted from Mount Sipylus, the water was said to be her tears. **Page 9.**

NISUS (nice-us) *Category:* mortal. *Family Status:* one d. Scylla. *Career:* King of Megara; lost war against Minos by

treachery of Scylla who stole his magic lock of hair; killed by Minos; turned into an eagle. *Personality:* aggressive and not very lovable. *Distinguishing Features:* purple lock of hair. *Supernatural Attributes:* possession of magic lock of hair. **Page 25.**

NORTH WIND see **BOREAS**

NYMPHS (nimfs) *Category:* demi-goddesses; see **NAIADS, DRYADS, NEREIDS.** *Career:* spirits of woodland and water; sometimes followers of Dionysus; often chased or loved by mortals or gods; see DAPHNE. *Distinguishing Features:* lovely women; to be found near water, trees or mountains, depending on type. *Supernatural Attributes:* long life.

Nymph

ODYSSEUS (oh-**dee**-see-us) *Roman:* Ulysses. *Category:* mortal. *Family Status:* s. of Laertes; m. Penelope; one s. Telemachus; lo. of Circe; several s. with her. *Career:* reluctant soldier – feigned madness to avoid going to Troy, but made to go in the end; once there, fought bravely; protected Achilles's body after his death; quarrelled with Ajax over Achilles's armour; thought up trick of Wooden Horse; displeased the gods by destructive behaviour after defeat of Troy; suffered mishaps and adventures on his way home – voyages of Odysseus became renowned; he had to throw out the nobles who had taken over his court in his absence; killed by men belonging to his and Circe's son – he had come looking for his father, who thought he was a raider and attacked. *Personality:* home-loving; brave when required; cunning; quick-witted, crafty. *Associations:* Homer's story of his adventures is called The Odyssey. **Pages 46, 47.**

OEDIPUS (ee-dip-puss) *Category:* mortal. *Family Status:* s. of Laius and Jocasta of Thebes; m. Jocasta; several children including d. Antigone. *Career:* bad start – abandoned as a baby to die because of Oracle predicting he would kill his father and marry his mother; he survived, was brought up in court at Corinth; as an adult, met Laius without knowing who he was, quarrelled with him and killed him; answered the riddle of the Sphinx – Thebans gave him the throne and Jocasta for a wife in gratitude; the Oracle was then fulfilled; his real identity revealed by Tiresias, the seer; horrified, Oedipus struck out his eyes and became an outcast, accompanied by Antigone; died near Athens and was buried by Theseus. *Personality:* noble and brave but ill-fated; good ruler; intellectual. *Associations:* Sigmund Freud, called a son's love of his mother and jealousy of his father an "Oedipus complex". **Page 29.**

ORACLE (or-ick-ull) Message from the gods; esp. associated with Apollo at Delphi. **Page 16.**

OREITHYIA (or-**eeth**-yee-a) *Category:* mortal. *Family Status:* d. of King Erechtheus of Athens; m. Boreas, the North Wind; several sons. *Career:* Boreas fell in love with her and carried her off one day while she was out dancing; their sons became Argonauts. *Personality:* good-natured; loving wife. **Page 30.**

ORESTES (or-**rest**-eez) *Category:* mortal. *Family Status:* s. of Agamemnon and Clytemnestra; m. Hermione. *Career:* family cursed by behaviour of ancestors (see **TANTALUS, PELOPS**); brought up away from home; returned after Oracle told him to avenge Agamamnon, who had been murdered by Clytemnestra; urged on by his sister, Electra, he killed Clytemnestra; was tormented by the Erinyes and driven to wandering round Greece; attempted to kill Helen of Troy; demanded trial by the gods – found to have suffered enough, but still tormented by Erinyes; Oracle then sent him to land of Taurians; he was captured and about to be sacrificed but saved by his sister, Iphigenia, presumed dead, but actually a priestess of Artemis among the Taurians; finally, the curse was lifted and he lived normal married life. *Personality:* unwilling hero; prefers quiet life; bad-temper caused by torment from Erinyes. *Distinguishing Features:* accompanied by Erinyes at all times during his atonement. **Pages 44, 45.**

ORION (or-**eye**-on) *Category:* demi-god. *Family Status:* lo. of Eos; lo. of Artemis. *Career:* brilliant hunter; came to sticky end, due to disrespect for goddesses who favoured him; abandoned Eos to hunt with Artemis, thereby annoying Apollo; Mother Earth sent giant scorpion to chase him; Apollo tricked Artemis into shooting him; attempts to have him revived by Asclepius failed; Artemis transformed him into the star-sign Orion. *Personality:* ladies' man; fickle lover; arrogant. *Distinguishing Features:* dashing good looks; hunting gear, especially sword-belt. *Associations:* constellation Orion is still followed across the sky by star-group Scorpio, the scorpion. **Page 29.**

ORPHEUS (or-**fee**-us) *Category:* mortal. *Family Status:* said to be s. of one of the Muses; m. Eurydice. *Career:* excellent musician on the lyre; accompanied Argonauts; played non-violent but critical role in obtaining golden

Orpheus

fleece by playing lullaby to dragon-serpent guard; also prevented loss of ship to the sirens by playing to drown their singing; tragic loss of his wife by snake-bite led him to venture to Underworld to get her back; by playing soothing music, he made a bargain with Pluto and was allowed to take her home, but broke his part of the bargain by looking over his shoulder before Eurydice had left the Underworld and she had to go back; horrible death when torn to shreds by Maenads for refusing to play happy music. *Personality:* artistic, musical; courageous but non-violent; rather sad. *Distinguishing*

Features: always carried his lyre. *Supernatural Attributes:* musical gift from the gods. *Associations:* birds said to sing more sweetly on the spot where he was killed. **Pages 31, 33.**

ORTHRUS (or-thruss) *Category:* monster. *Family Status:* s. of Echidne; fa. of Sphinx and Nemean Lion (mo. Echidne). *Career:* guarding cattle of Geryon; killed by Heracles. *Personality:* v. fierce. *Distinguishing Features:* 2-headed dog. **Page 38.**

PALLAS (pal-ass) *Category:* demi-goddess. *Family Status:* closely associated with Athene. *Career:* fight-practice partner and friend of Athene; killed accidentally by Athene; Athene called herself Pallas Athene to show her sorrow. *Personality:* noble; a good friend. **Page 15.**

PAN (pan) *Roman:* Faunus. *Category:* god. *Family Status:* s. of Hermes; lo. of Syrinx, a nymph. *Career:* god of nature, shepherds, herds and flocks; pursued Syrinx, who escaped him by being turned into a bed of reeds, from which he made pipes to play on; induces panic; unreasonable fear – especially outside or in the country. *Personality:* pleasure-seeking; prone to be over-amorous; frightening if disturbed. *Distinguishing Features:* man's body, goat's legs; sometimes given horns. *Supernatural Attributes:* immortality. **Page 5.**

Pan

PANDORA (pan-door-a) *Category:* demi-goddess. *Family Status:* created by Zeus; m. Epimetheus. *Career:* sent by Zeus to trick Epimetheus and punish mankind for accepting the gift of fire from Prometheus; she opened jar given her by Zeus, releasing all the evils into the world. *Personality:* incurably curious. *Supernatural Attributes:* immortality. **Page 21.**

PARIS (pa-riss) *Category:* human. *Family Status:* s. of Priam and Hecuba; lo. of Helen. *Career:* Trojan prince; destined to cause downfall of Troy – as predicted by the Oracle; he was abandoned to die as a baby, but survived; brought up by herdsman; chosen by Zeus to judge which was loveliest out of Hera, Athene and Aphrodite; chose Aphrodite and was promised the most beautiful woman in the world as his wife; offended Hera and Athene, which proved disastrous; as an adult, returned to Troy; his true identity was revealed and he was welcomed; went to Sparta on his father's business, saw Helen, fell in love and carried her off to Troy; Greeks stormed after to get her back, triggering start of the Trojan War; shot Achilles; was killed by archer, Philoctetes; Troy lost, so Paris did cause its ruin. *Personality:* rash and headstrong; susceptible to pretty women; sometimes said to be cowardly. *Supernatural Attributes:* had Aphrodite's protection but the disfavour of Hera and Athene working against him. *Distinguishing Features:* very good-looking. **Page 40.**

PATROCLUS (pat-rock-luss) *Category:* mortal. *Career:* Greek hero against the Trojans; great friend of Achilles; killed by Hector while impersonating Achilles to try and rally the discouraged Greeks. *Personality:* honourable; self-sacrificing. **Page 42.**

PEGASUS (peg-a-suss) *Category:* supernatural animal. *Family Status:* offspring of Poseidon and Medusa. *Career:* borrowed by hero, Bellerophon; helped him kill the Chimaera; took part in wars on behalf of King of Lycia; misused by Bellerophon in attempt to fly to Olympus; used by Zeus as instrument of Bellerophon's downfall; carries thunderbolts for Zeus. *Personality:* good-natured, obedient; neutrally loyal to any master – danger of being used to evil ends. *Distinguishing Features:* a horse with shining white coat; wings. *Supernatural Attributes:* flying ability.

Pegasus

PELEUS (pee-lyoos) *Category:* mortal. *Family Status:* m. Thetis; seven s., youngest was Achilles. *Career:* picked out by Zeus to marry the nereid, Thetis; had to catch her; found her and seized her; held on even while she changed shape and she eventually agreed to marry him; interrupted Thetis while making Achilles immortal, causing him to have one vulnerable spot – his heel. *Personality:* brave; persistent. **Page 23.**

PELIAS (pee-lee-ass) *Category:* mortal. *Family Status:* uncle to Jason; three d. *Career:* King of Iolcus after taking throne from Jason's father; sent Jason on quest for golden fleece, hoping he would not return; met violent death at the hands of his daughters, who were tricked by Medea into boiling him in a cauldron. *Personality:* ambitious; sly; sometimes underhand. **Pages 32, 33.**

PELOPS (pell-ops) *Category:* mortal. *Family Status:* s. of Tantalus; m. Hippodamia. *Career:* killed by his father and served to the gods at a feast; revived by gods and given ivory shoulder to replace one eaten by Demeter; helped by Poseidon to win chariot race for Hippodamia's hand against her father; renewed curse on his family by ingratitude to charioteer, Myrtilus, who also helped. *Personality:* daring, but egotistical; believes in taking what he wants; ungrateful. *Distinguishing Features:* ivory shoulder. *Supernatural Attributes:* favour of the gods after his mistreatment by his father. **Page 49**

PENELOPE (pen-ell-oh-pee) *Category:* mortal. *Family Status:* m. Odysseus; one s. Telemachus. *Career:* unhappily for her, Odysseus was away for twenty years, at the Trojan War and sailing home afterwards so she coped alone; was pressured by nobles to marry one of them; avoided this by saying she had to finish a piece of weaving first – she wove all day and then

unpicked it at night so it was never finished; the trick was uncovered, and she was about to give in, when Odysseus returned; another short period of happiness followed, before Odysseus's death. *Personality:* loving wife and mother; famed for her fidelity; ingenious. **Pages 46, 47.**

PENTHEUS (pen-thyoos) *Category:* mortal. *Family Status:* s. of Agave. *Career:* King of Thebes; foolishly attempted to prevent his mother worshipping Dionysus because he disapproved; imprisoned Dionysus and was persuaded to go and watch Agave and the Maenads perform their rites; the women saw him and tore him apart – his mother ripped his head off. *Personality:* domineering – especially over women; foolish enough to oppose the gods. **Page 19.**

PERSEPHONE (per-seff-on-nee) *Roman:* Proserpina. *Category:* goddess. *Family Status:* d. of Zeus and Demeter; m. Pluto; lo. of Adonis. *Career:* helped her mother care for harvests and growing things until Pluto grabbed her to be his bride; very unhappy in Underworld; eventually found by Demeter, but could not leave Underworld permanently because she had eaten pomegranate seeds from Pluto's garden; special dispensation from Zeus to spend half the year with Pluto and half with Demeter; living things die in sorrow when she is away – the winter season; argued with Aphrodite over Adonis, leading to his death. *Personality:* rather sad and severe when in the Underworld; gay and happy when with Demeter. *Distinguishing Features:* represents spring and new growth. *Supernatural Attributes:* immortality. **Page 11.**

PERSEUS (per-syoos) *Category:* mortal. *Family Status:* s. of Zeus and Danae; m. Andromeda. *Career:* set afloat with his mother, because of prediction that he would kill his grandfather; cared for by King Polydictes on Seriphos; challenged by Polydictes to kill Medusa, the Gorgon, and succeeded with the help of the gods; saved Andromeda from a sea-monster and married her; prophesy came true when he accidentally killed his grandfather in a discus-throwing contest. *Personality:* protective of his mother; keen for adventure; bold and brave. *Supernatural Attributes:* was lent magic reflective shield, Hermes's winged sandals, Pluto's helmet of invisibility and a sickle by the gods. **Page 24.**

PHAEDRA (feed-ra) *Category:* mortal. *Family Status:* d. of Minos and Pasiphae; sister of Ariadne; m. Theseus. *Career:* second wife to Theseus; meanly claimed her step-son, Hippolytus, had attacked her, causing Theseus to ask Poseidon to punish him; Hippolytus was killed, Theseus found out he was innocent and Phaedra hanged herself for fear of the consequences. *Personality:* jealous; unscrupulous. **Page 25.**

PHAETHON (feeth-on) *Category:* god. *Family Status:* s. of Helios. *Career:* probably would have taken over chariot of the sun from his father when mature, but insisted on having a go at the reins while inexperienced; he lost control and had to be struck down by Zeus to save the Earth; created Sahara Desert where he burned the Earth; mourned by his special friend, Cycnus. *Personality:* boastful; overconfident. **Page 26.**

PHILOCTETES (fill-**lock**-tee-teez) *Category:* mortal. *Career:* friend of Heracles; famous archer, he was given Heracles's bow when Heracles was taken to Olympus; set off for Troy with the Greeks; received snake bite on the way – wound would not heal so he was left behind; after death of Achilles, Odysseus came back begging for his help; he refused until visited in a dream by Heracles, telling him he would be healed if he helped; went to Troy and gave new hope to the troops; killed Paris; Greeks went on to win the war. *Personality:* proud; easily offended. **Page 43.**

PHINEUS (**fin**-ee-us) *Category:* mortal. *Career:* blind king and seer; life made a misery by the Harpies; visited by Jason and Argonauts; they drove the Harpies off in return for his help in getting past the Clashing Rocks. *Personality:* wise, shrewd. *Supernatural Attributes:* seeing the future. **Page 32.**

PHORCYS (**for**-sis) *Category:* god. *Family Status:* four d. Gorgons and Scylla. *Career:* sea-god; daughters turned into monsters by Athene. *Supernatural Attributes:* immortality. **Page 15.**

PHRIXUS (**fricks**-us) *Category:* mortal. *Family Status:* s. of Athamas and Nephele. *Career:* escaped sacrifice planned by his step-mother, Ino, on a golden ram sent by Hera; flew on ram's back to Colchis where he sacrificed it to Zeus; its fleece was hung in a sacred grove and guarded by a dragon serpent; Jason later went in search of the fleece. *Personality:* noble; respectful. **Page 25.**

PHYLLIS (**fill**-iss) *Category:* mortal. *Family Status:* due to m. Acamas. *Career:* waited for Acamas after he went to Trojan War; pined until she was about to die; Athene took pity and turned her into an almond tree; when Acamas retured he kissed the trunk of the tree and it blossomed, although the leaves were not yet out; the almond has flowered before its leaves appear ever since. *Personality:* faithful; sad. *Distinguishing Features:* took shape of an almond tree after her transformation. **Page 30.**

PINDAR Real person who wrote about the myths. He lived from 518-438 BC.

PIRITHOUS (pier-**rith**-o-us) *Category:* mortal. *Family Status:* s. of Ixion. King of Lapiths. *Career:* great friend and companion of Theseus; led him into scrapes; attempt to kidnap Persephone from Underworld ended in them being tied in chains of forgetfulness; left behind when Theseus rescued by Heracles. *Personality:* reckless to the point of foolishness; headstrong; bad influence. **Page 37.**

PLUTO (**ploo**-toe) *Roman:* Dis Pater. *Category:* god. *Family Status:* s. of Cronos and Rhea; m. Persephone. *Career:* swal-

lowed by his father at birth; rescued by Zeus; helped fight and defeat Cronos; given the Underworld as his kingdom; kidnapped Persephone against her will and married her. *Personality:* gloomy and frightening. *Distinguishing Features:* extremely rich - owns all precious metals and jewels. *Supernatural Attributes:* immortality; helmet of invisiblity that can be lent to mortals. *Associations:* planet named after him. **Pages 9, 10, 11, 27.**

POLYDEUCES (poll-ee-**dyoo**-seez) *Roman:* Pollux. *Category:* demi-god. *Family Status:* s. of Zeus and Leda; twin to Castor. *Career:* see **CASTOR**. *Personality:* heroic; strong family ties. *Supernatural Attributes:* immortality.

POLYDICTES (poll-ee-**dick**-teez) *Category:* mortal. *Family Status:* wanted to m. Danae. *Career:* King of Seriphos; rescued Danae and Perseus from the sea and looked after them; wished to marry Danae but was hindered by Perseus so suggested he attempt to kill Medusa; was about to force Danae to marry him when Perseus returned, with Medusa's head; Perseus took the head out and showed it to him and his courtiers and they turned to stone. *Personality:* generous; somewhat insensitive to the feelings of others. **Page 24.**

POLYPHEMUS (poll-ee-**fee**-muss) *Category:* Cyclops. *Family Status:* s. of Poseidon; descendent of the Cyclopes. *Career:* lived on Sicily; reared sheep to eat; captured Odysseus when he visited; blinded by Odysseus, who then escaped; called on Poseidon to curse Odysseus. *Personality:* dour; unfriendly; not sympathetic to humans. *Distinguishing Features:* giant stature; only one eye in the middle of his forehead. *Supernatural Attributes:* great strength. **Page 46.**

POSEIDON (poss-**eye**-don) *Roman:* Neptune. *Category:* god. *Family Status:* s. of Cronos and Rhea; m. Amphitrite; one s. Polyphemus (mo. possibly a Cyclops); sometimes said to be fa. of Bellerophon. *Career:* swallowed by his father at birth; rescued by Zeus; fought with Zeus against the Titans; given the Ocean as his kingdom; controlled storms and sea-monsters – drove Odysseus off-course, sent monster to devour Andromeda and a great wave to kill Hippolytus. *Personality:* less sociable than most other gods; does not mix with mortals much; powerful vengeance if angered. *Distinguishing Features:* three-pronged fork or Triton, made by Hephaestos. *Supernatural Attributes:* immortality; controlling the waves; causing earthquakes. *Associations:* called Earth-Shaker – Greeks assumed he made the Earth move in the same way he made the sea move. **Page 11.**

PRIAM (**pry**-am) *Category:* mortal. *Family Status:* m. many children incl. Hecuba; two s. Hector, Paris; one d. Cassandra. *Career:* King of Troy; sent Paris to Sparta to negotiate release of his sister, Hesione, who was their prisoner; lost Troy and was killed in the Trojan War. *Personality:* power-seeking; competitive, especially with Greeks.

PROMETHEUS (prom-ee-**thee**-us) *Category:* Titan. *Family Status:* s. of Uranus and Mother Earth; m. Hesione; one s. Deucalion. *Career:* fought with Zeus against Cronos; tutor to Athene; was asked to create a race to live on Earth by Zeus; created humans; tricked Zeus into accepting the worst part of a sacrifice, so mortals could have the good part; defied Zeus to give fire to mankind; was punished by a terrible torture – he was chained to a rock and an eagle was sent to tear out his liver; his liver was renewed every day and torn out again and again; eventually rescued by Heracles. *Personality:* great strength of character; wise, thoughtful. *Supernatural Attributes:* immortality. **Pages 20, 21.**

PROTEUS (**pro**-tee-us) see **BELLEROPHON**.

PSYCHE (**sye**-kee) *Category:* mortal, becoming goddess. *Family Status:* m. Eros. *Career:* lived happily with her sisters until carried off by Eros, who visited her secretly; urged by her sisters, she lit a lamp to see who her lo. was; Eros disappeared and was forbidden to return by Aphrodite; she tried to appease Aphrodite by performing impossible tasks – helped each time by Eros; at last Zeus took pity, calmed Aphrodite and made Psyche immortal so she could marry Eros. *Personality:* easily influenced; vain; tenderhearted. *Distinguishing Features:* very beautiful; butterfly wings. *Supernatural Attributes:* immortality. *Associations:* "psyche" means "breath" and was used to refer to the non-physical part of a person – the mind or spirit; so "psychology" is the study of the human mind. **Page 31.**

PYGMALION (pig-**mail**-ee-on) *Category:* mortal. *Family Status:* m. Galatea. *Career:* sculptor; worshipper of Aphrodite; could not find true love so made statue of his ideal woman; he fell in love with the statue – rescued by Aphrodite who brought the statue to life so they could marry. *Personality:* artistic; determined; idealistic. *Distinguishing Features:* usually found with his sculptor's tools. *Associations:* George Bernard Shaw wrote a play called "Pygmalion", about a man who tried to mould a girl into his perfect woman. **Page 13.**

PYLADES (**pie**-lad-eez) *Category:* mortal. *Family Status:* cousin to Orestes; m. Electra. *Career:* accompanied Orestes to land of Taurians. *Personality:* brave; good friend. **Pages 44, 45.**

PYRRHA (**pir**-ra) *Category:* mortal. *Family Status:* d. of Epimetheus; m. Deucalion; ancestor of all mortal women. *Career:* see **DEUCALION**. *Personality:* worthy survivor. **Page 21.**

PYTHON (**pie**-thon) *Category:* monster. *Family Status:* Hera's servant. *Career:* obeyed Hera; was set on Leto, when Hera found out about her affair with Zeus; killed at Delphi by Apollo. *Personality:* vindictive. *Supernatural Attributes:* it was a gigantic snake. *Associations:* priestess of Apollo at Delphi called Pythoness. **Page 16.**

RHEA (**ree**-a) *Category:* Titaness. *Family Status:* d. of Uranus and Mother Earth; m. her brother, Cronos; three s. Zeus, Poseidon, Pluto; three d. Hestia, Demeter, Hera. *Career:* Queen of the Titans; unhappy marriage with Cronos because he swallowed all her children, due to prophesy that one of them would depose him; she saved Zeus, who rescued the rest of them; always shown great respect after Zeus and the New Gods took over. *Personality:* strong-willed; clever. *Supernatural Attributes:* immortality. **Page 8.**

SATYRS (**sat**-ires) *Category:* demigods. *Career:* spirits of nature; worshipping Dionysus; drinking and chasing nymphs. *Personalities:* mischievous troublemakers; extremely amorous. *Distinguishing Features:*

Satyr

young, handsome men with ears and tail of a horse. **Page 18.**

SCYLLA (**sill**-a) *Category:* mortal. *Family Status:* d. of King Nisus of Megara. *Career:* trapped in Megara while under siege by Minos; fell in love with Minos from the ramparts; wanted him to win the battle, so stole her father's magic lock of hair and took it to him; he accepted it but rejected Scylla for her treacherous behaviour; tried to swim after Minos but attacked by her father's spirit in the form of an eagle and drowned. *Personality:* romantic to a foolish degree; thoughtless. **Page 25.**

SCYLLA *Category:* monster. *Family Status: Career:* d. of Phorcys; loved by Poseidon; turned into a monster by jealous Amphitrite.

Scylla

killing sailors and wrecking ships; Odysseus was one of the few that escaped. *Personality:* deliberately evil; anti-mortals; noisy and terrifying. *Distinguishing Features:* female; six heads; ring of snarling dogs round her waist; always found in the vicinity of Charybdis, the whirlpool. *Supernatural Attributes:* enormous capacity to harm mortals. **Page 47.**

SEASONS (**see**-zunz) *Category:* demigoddesses. *Career:* gatekeepers of Olympus; often attended goddesses; brought clothes and jewels to Aphrodite when she was brought to Cyprus. *Distinguishing Features:* three of them – Spring, Summer and Winter. *Supernatural Attributes:* immortality. **Page 12.**

SELENE (**sell**-ee-nee) *Category:* Titaness. *Family Status:* d. of Hyperion and Theia. *Career:* drove chariot of the moon; often confused with Artemis; was loved by Endymion, who was put in eternal sleep by Zeus so he could dream about her. *Personality:* distant; unapproachable. *Supernatural Attributes:* immortality.

SEMELE (**sem**-a-lee) *Category:* mortal. *Family Status:* d. of Cadmus; lo. of Zeus; one s. Dionysus (fa. Zeus). *Career:* while expecting Zeus's child, Hera persuaded her to insist on seeing his true form; struck dead when he appeared as lightning and blasted her; their son, Dionysus, was saved by Zeus and he took his mo. to Olympus. *Personality:* inquisitive; gullible. **Page 18.**

SILENUS (**sye**-leen-us) *Category:* demigod; satyr. *Career:* worshipping Dionysus; indulging himself in a good time; it was for looking after him when in a drunken stupor that Dionysus granted Midas a wish *Personality:* pleasure-seeking; irresponsible. *Distinguishing Features:* fat and old; often drunk; frequently seen riding an ass. **Page 18.**

SILVER RACE *Category:* mortal. *Family Status:* created by Zeus. *Career:* unsuccessful race made by Zeus to live on Earth to replace the Golden Race; turned out to be evil so were all destroyed by Zeus. *Personalities:* wilfully ' d. **Page 20.**

SIRENS (**sye**-runs) *Category:* monsters. *Career:* singing to lure sailors onto the jagged rocks where they lived and wrecking their ships; only Jason and Odysseus ever managed to escape – Odysseus actually heard their singing without dying by hav-

Siren

ing himself tied to the mast. *Personalities:* destructive; wicked. *Distinguishing Features:* very beautiful female faces and voices; bird-like bodies with wings and claws. *Supernatural Attributes:* their voices, which are irresistibly attractive to humans. **Pages 33, 47.**

SISYPHUS (**sis**-ee-fuss) *Category:* mortal. *Family Status:* s. of Aeolus. *Career:* was a friend of Zeus but betrayed secrets told him by the god; stole his brother's throne; seduced his niece; Zeus sent Pluto to take him to Tartarus; he tricked Pluto into trying on his own chains and made him prisoner, causing havoc, as no-one could die without Pluto to guide them to the Underworld; Ares was sent to rescue Pluto; Sisyphus was punished by being made to roll a boulder up a steep hill in Tartarus – each time he got to the top it rolled back down again so he could never complete his task. *Personality:* cunning; egotistical; ungrateful. **Page 27.**

SOPHOCLES (**soff**-oh-kleez) Real man. Wrote plays about the myths.

SOUTH WIND see **AUSTER**.

SPHINX (**sfincks**) *Category:* monster. *Family Status:* child of Orthrus and Echidne. *Career:* challenging humans to answer her riddle (see page 29) and killing them if they cannot; cor-

Sphinx

rect answer was "a man" – he crawls on all-fours when a weak baby, walks on his two legs when a strong youth and uses a stick as a third leg when feeble and old; given the correct answer by Oedipus; committed suicide in shame. *Personality:* evil; smug. *Distinguishing Features:* woman's head, lion's body, wings; to be found on the road to Thebes. *Associations:* Sphinxes feature in Egyptian myths, too, **Page 29.**

STYMPHALIAN BIRDS (stim-**fail**-ee-an birds) *Category:* monsters. *Career:* scavenging and disturbing the people of Stymphalus because of their great numbers. *Personalities:* greedy nuisances. *Distinguishing Features:* birds with bronze beaks, wings and claws. **Page 38.**

TALOS (**ta**-los) *Category:* monster. *Family Status:* servant to Minos. *Career:* made by Hephaestos; threw boulders to ward off strangers approaching Crete; killed when Medea took out the pin that held his life force in his body. *Distinguishing Features:* giant made of bronze; to be found striding round Crete. *Supernatural Attributes:* giant strength. **Page 33.**

TANTALUS (**tan**-ta-luss) *Category:* mortal. *Family Status:* s. of Zeus and a Titaness; two s. incl. Pelops; one d. Niobe. *Career:* initially great friend of the gods; ate ambrosia and nectar with them; invited them to a banquet where he dished up his son for them to eat, simply to see if they could tell what they were eating; he could not fool the gods and was punished in Tartarus by having food and drink placed near him but just out of reach; if he tried to stretch out for it, it moved away. *Personality:* consciously wicked; misused his privileged position. *Distinguishing Features:* eternally up to his neck in water in Tartarus. *Associations:* the word "tantalizing", used to describe something desirable but out of reach, comes from his name; **Page 27.**

TELEMACHUS (tell-e-**mack**-us) *Category:* mortal. *Family Status:* s. of Odysseus and Penelope. *Career:* grew up without his father, who was at Trojan War and then on his travels; protected his mother, but could not stop nobles bothering her and wasting his father's wealth; helped Odysseus once he returned and revealed who he was; stole the weapons of the nobles courting Penelope and helped kill them when they were defenceless. *Personality:* honorable and brave but inexperienced. **Pages 46, 47.**

THEMIS (**thee**-miss) *Category:* Titaness. *Family Status:* d. of Uranus and Mother Earth. *Career:* sent by Zeus to help Deucalion and Pyrrha found human race after the flood. *Supernatural Attributes:* immortality. **Page 21.**

THESEUS (**thee**-syoos) *Category:* mortal. *Family Status:* s. of Aegeus and Aethra; lo. of Ariadne; m. Hippolyte; m. Phaedra; one s. Hipplytus (mo. Hippolyte). *Career:* volunteered to go to Crete as one of the victims of the Minotaur; Ariadne fell in love with him and helped him; he killed the Minotaur and escaped with the other victims and Ariadne; left Ariadne behind on the way home, on Naxos; forgot to change the sails from black to white to heraldthe news that he was safe, causing his father to commit suicide in despair; became king and m. Hippolyte, who was killed in battle; lost his son due to wicked plots of second wife, Phaedra; disillusioned, he took to adventuring; led on madcap scheme to kidnap Persephone by Pirithous; caught by the gods and tied in chains of forgetfulness; rescued by Heracles; lost his kingdom, retired to Scyros; his body brought back to Athens and buried with honour after his ghost appeared and spurred the troops to victory at the battle of Marathon. *Personality:* good, courageous and bold in his youth; became reckless adventurer after tragic loss of his son. *Supernatural Attributes:* his love of Athens lived on after his death and his ghost was often said to appear to soldiers defending the city. **Pages 34, 36.**

THETIS (**thee**-tiss) *Category:* demi-goddess; nereid. *Family Status:* lo. of Zeus; m. Peleus; seven s., incl. Achilles. *Career:* Zeus wanted to marry her but did not because it was predicted that any son she had would be greater than its father, a risk Zeus could not take; Zeus sent Peleus to catch and marry her; she tried to escape by assuming different shapes but gave in eventually; Eris brought apple inscribed "For the fairest" to their wedding – cause of Trojan War; made six of her sons immortal, but Achilles was left with one vulnerable spot on his heel because she was interrupted by Peleus. *Distinguishing Features:* normal shape is a beautiful woman. *Supernatural Attributes:* shape-changing ability. **Page 23.**

TIRESIAS (tire-**ee**-see-us) *Category:* mortal. *Family Status:* blinded by Athene; became great seer; found out Oedipus's

true identity; gave Odysseus advice when visited by him in the Underworld. *Personality:* very knowledgeable; gives good advice. *Distinguishing Features:* an old man with a stick. *Supernatural Attributes:* telling the future. **Pages 29, 47.**

TITANS (**tie**-tans) *Family Status:* descendants of Uranus and Mother Earth. *Career:* were rulers of the world until revolt led by Zeus; after this, most of them were imprisoned in Tartarus; see **CRONOS, RHEA, PROMETHEUS, ATLAS.** *Personalities:* varied – some good, some bad. *Distinguishing Features:* giant size. *Supernatural Attributes:* immortality. **Page 8.**

TROS (**tross**) *Category:* mortal. *Family Status:* one s. Ganymede. *Career:* King of Troy, which was named after him.

TYNDAREUS (tin-**dar**-yoos) *Category:* mortal. *Family Status:* m. Leda; one s. Castor; one d. Clytemnestra. *Career:* king; cared for Leda's children by Zeus as well as his own offspring; chose Menelaus as husband for Helen; made Helen's suitors swear to support her husband. *Personality:* kind and generous; clever. **Page 41.**

URANUS (you-**rain**-us) *Category:* god. *Family Status:* s. of Mother Earth; m. Mother Earth; many children incl. giants, Cyclopes, Titans, Titanesses; fa. of Erinyes and Aphrodite. *Career:* he is the sky; he and Mother Earth produced all living things; he was displeased with some of them and imprisoned them in Tartarus; Mother Earth turned against him and encouraged Titans to rebel; defeated by Cronos with a sickle; where his blood fell on Earth, the Erinyes appeared; Aphrodite was born from the foam caused when his blood dropped in the ocean. *Personality:* heartless; cruel. *Supernatural Attri-*

butes: fathering monstrous offspring; immortality. *Associations:* planet named after him. **Page 8.**

VENUS (**vee**-nuss) see **APHRODITE.**

WEST WIND see **ZEPHYR.**

ZEPHYR (**zeff**-er) *Category:* god. *Family Status:* under the control of Aeolus. *Career:* West Wind; blew mild, warm winds as directed. *Distinguishing Features:* young, handsome man, sometimes with a serpent's tail. *Supernatural Attributes:* flying with the wind.

ZEUS (**zyoos**) *Roman:* Jupiter. *Category:* god. *Family Status:* s. of Cronos and Rhea; m. his sister, Hera and had one s. Ares, two d. Eris, Hebe; one d., Athene, born from his head; lo. of Semele, Io, Europa, Danae, Leda, Alcmene and many others; sons incl. Perseus (mo. Danae), Heracles (mo. Alcmene), Tantalus (mo. Titaness), Polydictes (mo. Leda), Minos, Rhadamanthys, Sarpedon (mo. Europa); daughters incl. Helen (mo. Leda). Career: saved by his mother from being swallowed at birth by Cronos; grew up safely and staged a rebellion; released his brothers and sisters; defeated Cronos and took over as King of the gods; ruled from Olympus; very fond of visiting the Earth and getting involved in human affairs. *Personality:* dominating; powerful; soft spot for pretty women; terrifying when angry. *Distinguishing features:* thunderbolts made by Cyclopes to be hurled when annoyed. *Supernatural Attributes:* immortality; all-powerful to do what he wants with mortals - strike them down, turn them into animals, cause the defeat of an army etc. *Associations:* eagle was his bird; oaks sacred to him. **Pages 9, 11, 22, 23.**

Mythological places

ASPHODEL FIELDS (**ass**-foe-dell fields) Part of the Underworld where most ordinary humans, who had done nothing especially bad or good, went when they died. A grey, misty place where people wandered around as shadows of their earthly selves. **Page 8.**

CHAOS (**kay**-oss) State of confusion before Earth came into existence. **Page 8.**

EARTH Where humans lived. The gods often visited Earth and intervened in people's lives. **Page 8.**

ELYSIAN FIELDS (ell-**iz**-ian fields) Area in the Underworld where people who were particularly good or heroic went when they died. A golden, blissful place where tired warriors could rest. **Page 8.**

HADES (**hay**-deez) Another name for the Underworld (see below). Also sometimes used as a name for Pluto, the god of the Underworld. **Page 8.**

ISLES OF THE BLESSED The most distant part of the Underworld. Only very favoured people went there. If you were

sent back to Earth by the gods to live another life three times and each time managed to be good enough to be sent to the Elysian Fields, you were then allowed to go to the Isles of the Blessed, from which you could never be recalled. **Page 8.**

LABYRINTH (**lab**-ee-rinth) Underground maze at Knossos, designed by Daedalus to keep the Minotaur in. **Page 34.**

MOUNT OLYMPUS see **OLYMPUS.**

OCEAN The Ancient Greeks believed that a continuous circle of water surrounded the land. This was the Ocean and was Poseidon's kingom. **Page 9.**

OLYMPUS (oh-**limp**-us) The high mountain where Zeus and the other gods lived (except for Pluto and Poseidon who lived in their own kingdoms). Originally supposed to be the real mountain of that name in Northern Greece but was eventually thought of as a more imaginary place high above the Earth. Each god and

goddess had his or her own palace on the mountain peak. No-one could go there without the express invitation of the gods. **Page 9.**

STYX (**sticks**) River you had to cross to enter the Underworld. the gods also swore oaths by the name of the Styx and any such oath was unbreakable. **Page 9.**

TARTARUS (**tar**-tar-us) Part of the Underworld where evil people were punished. They suffered horrible, eternal tortures, often designed for the individual by Zeus. Ruled by Pluto. **Page 8**

UNDERWORLD Pluto's kingdom. All humans went there when they died. It was underground and its entrance was a cave which was guarded by the three-headed dog, Cerberus. You also had to cross the River Styx in the boat belonging to the ferryman, Charon. Divided into three mains parts, the Asphodel Fields, Tartarus and the Elysian Fields (see the entries under these titles). The Isles of the Blessed were a special part of it (see above). **Page 8.**

ROMAN WHO'S WHO

This is a Who's Who of the gods and heroes that were most important to the Romans. Their earliest gods were simply powers. They prayed to them for help and had to pay them with offerings. They did not give them personalities or tell myths about them, like the Greeks.

Later, the Romans adopted a lot of the Greek myths and combined many of their gods with Greek ones. They usually kept the Roman name, though. In these cases, the Greek name is given next to the Roman one and you can look it up in the Greek Who's Who.

AENEAS: see **AENEAS.** Story of his journey to Italy with the Palladium after Trojan War (page 44) linked histories of Greece and Rome.

APOLLO: see **APOLLO.**

ASCANIUS (ass-cane-ee-us) *Category:* human. *Family Status:* s. of Aeneas. *Career:* taken from Troy by Aeneas when a baby; became king of Alba Longa, city founded by his father; also called Julus by Latin authors; Julian family claimed to be descended from him, so Julius Caesar claimed him, and his grandmother, Venus (Aphrodite), as ancestors. *Personality:* heroic; regal.

AURORA (or-**roar**-a) see **EOS.**

BONA DEA (**bone**-a **day**-a). *Category:* goddess. *Career:* fertility goddess; only worshipped by women.

BACCHAE (**back**-ee) see **MAENADS.**

BACCHUS (**back**-us): see **DIONYSUS.**

CACUS (**kak**-us). *Category:* giant. *Family Status:* s. of Vulcan (Hephaestos). *Career:* lived in cave on Palatine hill, outside Rome; stole cattle of Geryon from Hercules; Hercules traced them to Cacus' cave, dragged them out and killed Cacus. *Personality:* fiery, aggressive. *Supernatural Attributes:* breathes fire.

CASTOR (**cass**-tore) and **POLLUX** (**poll**-lux). See **CASTOR** and **POLYDEUCES.** Their ghosts seen in battle, leading the Roman army to victory.

CERES (**see**-reez): see **DEMETER.**

CUPID (**cue**-pid): see **EROS.**

DIANA (die-**an**-a): see **ARTEMIS.**

DIS PATER (**diss pate**-er): see **PLUTO.**

EMPERORS. *Category:* humans becoming gods. *Career:* ruled as emperors while alive; deified after death and worshipped; first god emperor was Augustus. *Supernatural Attributes:* gained immortality.

FAUNS (**fawns**) *Category:* supernatural beings. *Career:* followers of **FAUNUS;** mischievous; amorous; assoc. with Greek **SATYRS.** *Distinguishing Features:* men with goats' hind legs and horns.

FAUNUS (**fawn**-us): see **PAN.**

FLORA (**floor**-a) *Category:* goddess. *Career:* assoc. with flowers and spring; festival for her in April; assoc. with Greek Chloris, wife of Zephyrus, the West Wind. *Personality:* merry.

FORTUNA (for-**tune**-a) *Category:* goddess. *Career:* goddess of Fate; esp. important to emperors.

FURIES (**fyoor**-eez) see **ERINYES.**

HERCULES (**herk**-yoo-leez) see **HERACLES.**

ISIS (**eye**-sis) *Category:* foreign goddess. *Family Status:* m. Osiris; one s. Horus. *Career:* Egyptian goddess widely adopted in Roman Empire; had special initiation rites, processions and dances; Egyptian priests carried out ceremonies.

JANUS (**jane**-us) *Category:* god. *Career:* guardian of gateways; assoc. with good beginnings; first month of the year in calendar introduced by Julius Caesar called Januarius (January) after him; doors of his temple only closed when Rome at peace – quite rarely. *Distinguishing Features:* two faces pointing opposite ways.

JUNO (**joo**-no) see **HERA.**

JUPITER (**joo**-pit-er) see **ZEUS.**

LARES (**la**-raze) and **PENATES** (pen-**ah**-taze). *Category:* gods. *Career:* originally worshipped as gods of farms and crossroads; became protectors of the family, hearth and home; were worshipped at private shrines in houses.

MANES (**ma**-naze). *Category:* supernatural beings. *Career:* spirits of the dead; appeased by ceremonies at the grave.

MARS (**mars**): see **ARES.**

MERCURY (**mer**-cure-ee): see **HERMES.**

MINERVA (min-**erv**-a) see **ATHENE.**

MITHRAS (**mith**-rass) *Category:* foreign god. *Career:* Persian god, adopted by Roman soldiers; his worship spread throughout Roman Empire; men-only cult with secret rituals carried out underground or in caves. *Distinguishing Features:* always assoc. with a bull. *Supernatural Attributes:* offers immortality.

NEPTUNE (**nep**-tune): see **POSEIDON.**

POLLUX. See **CASTOR.**

PROSERPINA (prose-er-**peen**-a) see **PERSEPHONE.**

REMUS (**ree**-muss) *Category:* human. *Family Status:* twin s. of Rhea Silvia (a Vestal Virgin – see **VESTA** below – and descendant of Aeneas) and Mars. *Career:* exposed in basket on River Tiber to die with his twin, Romulus; washed up safely on shore near a fig tree and a cave called the Lupercal (Place of the Wolf); fed milk by a she-wolf; rescued and cared for by a shepherd; when grown up, built city of Rome on spot where rescue took place; killed by Romulus in an argument during the ceremony of the founding of Rome.

ROMULUS (**rom**-you-luss) *Category:* human. *Family Status:* twin s. of Rhea Silvia and Mars. *Career:* same fate in childhood as twin brother, Remus (see above); after killing Remus, he completed the city of Rome and ruled as its first king; deified after his death and associated with Quirinus, a god of war.

SATURN see **CRONOS.**

SILVANUS (sil-**vah**-nuss). *Category:* god. *Career:* god of fields, woods and flocks; feared by women in labour and children. *Distinguishing Features:* rather like **FAUNOS** and often confused with him.

SOL INVICTUS (**sol** in-**vick**-tuss) see **HELIOS.** *Associations:* The word "solar" meaning "of the sun" comes from his name.

SYBILS (**sib**-ills) *Category:* seeresses. *Career:* priestesses of Apollo; Sibyl at Cumae sold three books of prophecy to King Tarquin, which were consulted for advice and guidance by future kings. *Supernatural Attributes:* seeing future.

TERMINUS (**term**-in-us) *Category:* god. *Career:* god of boundaries; every boundary had a shrine to him.

ULYSSES (**yoo**-liss-eez) see **ODYSSEUS.**

VENUS (**vee**-nuss) see **APHRODITE.**

VESTA (**vest**-a) see **HEBTIA.** Sacred fire in her temple attended by priestesses called Vestal Virgins, who were supposed to remain chaste.

VULCAN (**vull**-can) see **HEPHAESTOS.**

NORSE
MYTHS AND LEGENDS

CONTENTS

Additional design by Graham Round

Additional illustration by Joe McEwan, Mark Duffin and Jan Nesbitt

Consultant checker Chris Jackson

BEFORE YOU START

This part of the book is about the most famous gods and goddesses in Norse Mythology and their exploits. There are more myths than there is room for here, but you will get a taste of the world of the Norse gods.

About this part of the book

The gods are introduced on pages 74-85 and the best-known stories about them are on pages 86-103.

To help you understand the people who told the myths, you can find out about the history and religion of the Norsemen on pages 68-71. The map on page 67 shows their travels.

Starting on page 104 is a detailed Who's Who reference section of characters and monsters that appear in the myths. In the book their names appear in bold print the first time they occur in a story. Use the Who's Who to find out about Trolls, Dwarfs, Elves and other creatures or to find characters for your own role-playing games.

What is a myth?

It is difficult to define exactly what a myth is. It is usually considered to be a work of the imagination that has a religious significance. Some appear to try to explain things which would probably be described scientifically today, such as how the world began.

Others describe the gods' behaviour, which was an exaggerated version of the lifestyle of the Norsemen and may have been meant to inspire courage. It is impossible at this distance of time to know exactly why particular gods were worshipped.

Where the myths came from

In this book the Norse Myths are taken to be mainly from Scandinavia and Iceland, although Norsemen also lived in Germany, Russia and further afield (see map opposite). People in different areas created local myths of their own.

The only myth in this book that was not wholly Scandinavian is the story of **Sigurd** and the Nibelungs (see pages 98-99). This came from Germany, but was adopted by the Scandinavians. It is famous due to Richard Wagner's opera cycle, *Der Ring des Nibelungen*.

How the myths were told

The Norse Myths were passed on by word of mouth. There were people who were especially good at telling them, called bards. They would entertain the lords in their halls on the long, winter evenings.

The myths were often composed as poems, which probably helped the bards to remember them. Those that were in prose were called sagas.

They were told in a typically Norse style, using tricks such as putting words with a similar sound together to create an effect.

There were traditional ways to describe each god, which came up again and again.

Characters had lots of nicknames – **Odin,** king of the gods, had as many as fifty, such as One-Eyed and Allfather.

The Norsemen were very keen on their ancestry. Long lists of heroes were often included in the stories. Objects were often given names, too.

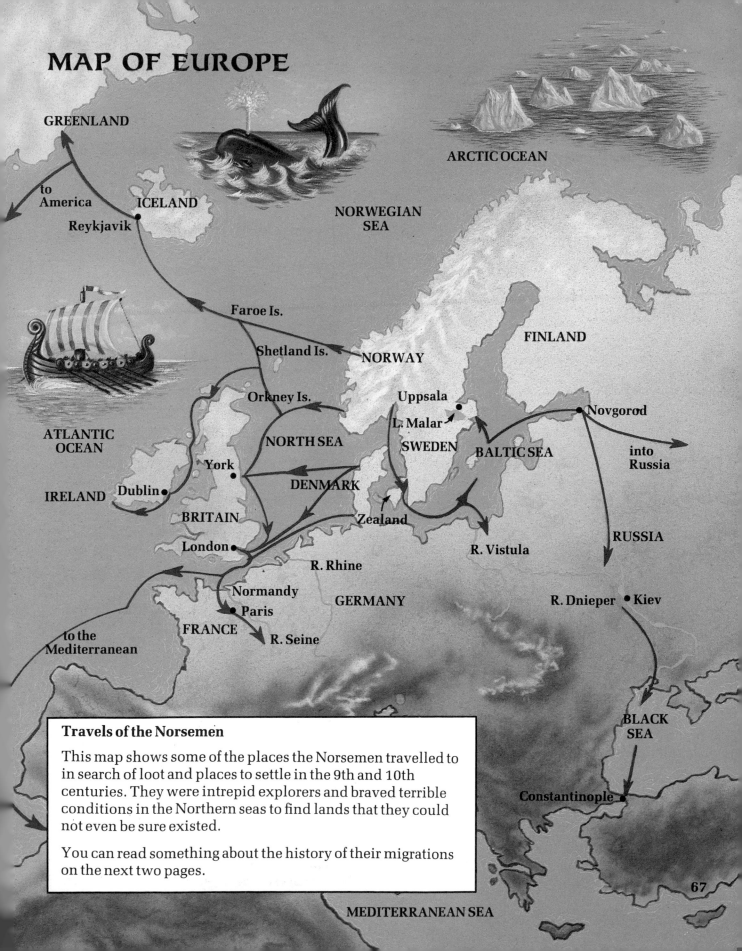

MAP OF EUROPE

GREENLAND

to America

Reykjavik

ICELAND

ARCTIC OCEAN

NORWEGIAN SEA

Faroe Is.

Shetland Is.

NORWAY

FINLAND

Orkney Is.

Uppsala

L. Malar

SWEDEN

BALTIC SEA

Novgorod

into Russia

ATLANTIC OCEAN

NORTH SEA

York

DENMARK

IRELAND

Dublin

BRITAIN

Zealand

RUSSIA

London

R. Vistula

R. Rhine

Normandy

GERMANY

R. Dnieper

Kiev

Paris

FRANCE

to the Mediterranean

R. Seine

BLACK SEA

Travels of the Norsemen

This map shows some of the places the Norsemen travelled to in search of loot and places to settle in the 9th and 10th centuries. They were intrepid explorers and braved terrible conditions in the Northern seas to find lands that they could not even be sure existed.

You can read something about the history of their migrations on the next two pages.

Constantinople

67

MEDITERRANEAN SEA

HISTORY OF THE NORSEMEN

The Norsemen did not use writing until very late in their history. They passed their myths on by word of mouth for centuries until they were written down by people such as the Icelander Snorri Sturlusson in the 12th century AD. By this time, Iceland had become Christian and the new religion probably influenced how Snorri told the ancient sagas. Below you can read about the beginnings of the Norsemen.

The Germani

About 1000 BC, there was a group of tribes in North-West Europe who shared similar languages and customs. At one time they were probably all closely related and may have come from further east. They slowly spread into South Scandinavia, the Baltic islands, Jutland and the North German Plain. The wider apart they spread, the more different they became.

This is a Runestone. Runes were magic symbols that were the earliest Norse form of writing.

The history of these people is not well-known because they did not record it. What we do know about them is mostly from Roman accounts. These are usually unfavourable, as the Romans considered the tribes to be barbaric enemies. They lumped all the tribes together and called them 'Germani', although there were really three distinct groups:

East Germani

These tribes lived around the River Vistula (see map on page 3). They included the Goths, Visigoths and Vandals. They migrated towards the Black Sea and came up against the Romans in the 4th century AD.

West Germani

These people spread south and west towards the Rivers Rhine and Danube. They clashed with the Romans in the 2nd century AD. They were the ancestors of the Germans, the Franks who populated parts of France, and the Angles and Saxons who later invaded Britain.

North Germani or Vikings

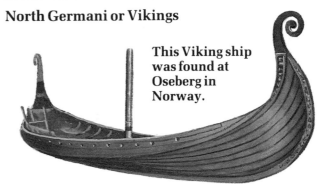

This Viking ship was found at Oseberg in Norway.

Another group moved north into Scandinavia and became the North or Norse men. The period of their history between about the years AD 700 and 1070 is often called the Viking Era and the Norsemen at this time are known as Vikings. Viking is a Norse word, whose meaning is not clear, but it may refer to the adventurous, seafaring lifestyle of the time.

The Viking life

Norsemen were originally farmers and fishermen but the lands they inhabited were so rugged and infertile that they had to find other means to live.

Traders used sledges like this one.

They were expert sailors and some of them became rich through trading. Others hired themselves out to foreign kings – the Emperors of Constantinople were proud of their Viking bodyguard, called the Varangian Guard.

Some found the rich monasteries on the Scottish islands and the coasts of England and Ireland too tempting and turned to piracy. They terrorized the coasts and gained a bloodthirsty reputation.

This is the handle of a Viking sword.

The spread of the Norsemen

The Vikings soon spread further west looking for conquests. They reached Iceland (AD 874), Greenland (AD 982) and even North America (about AD 1000). They explored via the rivers of Europe too, into France, Germany, Russia and as far as Constantinople. The riches of the Mediterranean cities also invited Viking raids.

Viking raiders and traders started to settle in the lands they visited and often made their mark where they settled. A Dane called Canute became King of England between AD 1016 and 1035. Another, Rollo, was made a duke in France. His duchy was Normandy, meaning North men's land.

These are Viking coins from York in England.

The importance of Iceland

Iceland left its mark in the Norse Myths because this is where they were first written down. The main sources are the works known as the *Verse Edda* and the *Prose Edda*. The *Verse Edda* consists of poems about the myths by different poets. The *Prose Edda* is the work of Snorri Sturlusson, who lived from 1179-1241. It is a guide for poets and includes many of the myths.

The Icelandic landscape and climate seem to have had an influence on the myths. The extremes of ice and fire that appear in the stories recall the snow and ice, volcanoes and hot geysers of Iceland.

This necklace is typical of those described in the Norse Myths.

The coming of Christianity

Christianity took a long time to reach these northern tribes. Missionaries first appeared in Denmark in the 9th century AD and the word took about 200 years to spread. As Christianity was accepted, so the old gods and goddesses died out.

By the end of the 11th century AD the Norsemen had stopped their Viking activities and become part of the pattern of Medieval Europe in the kingdoms of Norway, Sweden and Denmark.

This early Christian church still stands at Heddal, in Norway. It is made of wood and is called a stave church. It is thought that the pagan temples of the Vikings may have been built in a similar way.

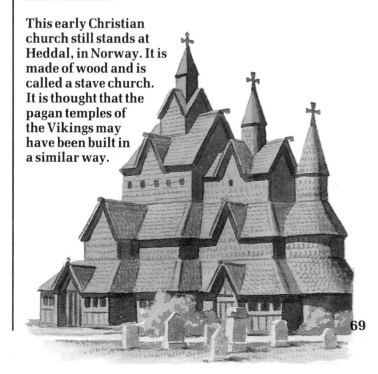

MYTHS AND RELIGION

The Norse Myths are stories concerning the gods of the Norsemen, and formed part of their religion. They illustrate the behaviour that was admired or condemned by the gods, although they do not provide definite rules or guidelines as in religious works like the Bible or the Koran.

This is a carved memorial stone. It shows Odin, King of the gods, with his servants the Valkyries. Below them is a Viking ship.

What religion meant to the Norsemen

It is hard to know exactly what the gods meant to the Vikings, or how they worshipped them, since they did not write anything down. They built temples, but very few remains have been found as they were made of wood and only the foundations have survived.

Outsiders who came into contact with them gave horrified reports of animal and even human sacrifices, but they seem to have made no effort to understand the meaning of the ceremonies.

This richly carved wooden cart may have been used in religious ceremonies.

The gods and goddesses

Freyja was goddess of love and beauty. This pendant is an image of her.

We do know that there was a large number of gods and goddesses, divided into two types, the **Aesir** and the **Vanir.** They represented different aspects of life and people worshipped whichever ones were most relevant to them.

The Vanir were fertility gods and important to farmers, while the Aesir were warriors, worshipped by fighting men and kings. Some people think that the Vanir were the first Norse gods and that the Aesir were introduced later. The myth about the war between the gods (see page 86) may represent the struggle for popularity between the two types.

Apart from temples, natural places such as a clearing, a waterfall or a stone were sometimes dedicated to a god.

What the gods were like

The Norse gods were very like the Norsemen. They fought, married and loved adventures. They felt human emotions such as jealousy and could behave in a most ungodlike way.

They were not immortal which meant they could be truly heroic since their lives could be in danger. In fact, most of them are doomed to die at **Ragnarok**, or the end of the world (see page 102).

Here is a bronze statue of Thor the thunder god.

Giants, Trolls and Dwarfs

Apart from the gods, the Norsemen believed the world was populated by all sorts of strange creatures, some good and some evil. **Elves** inhabited almost every wood and stream and could be mischievous or helpful. **Dwarfs** lived underground and it was said that they could

The god Thor was famous for his hammer. Pendants like this one were worn to ward off evil spirits.

not stand the daylight. If they were caught outside at dawn they turned to stone, which explains the scattered rocks on the valley floors. **Kobolds** were small human-shaped creatures who frequented barns and stables and could be helpful if treated well.

Trolls and **Giants** were both very large and dangerous and lived in the mountains.

Priests and seeresses

There were priests and priestesses who were thought to have special powers to talk to the gods, but most religious rites could be performed by chiefs or kings when necessary. The religion does not appear to have had fixed ceremonies and priests and priestesses were not set aside from ordinary people.

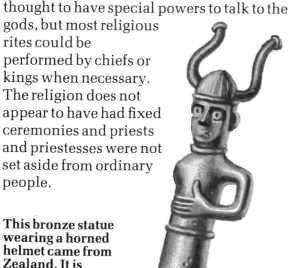

This bronze statue wearing a horned helmet came from Zealand. It is probably of one of the gods.

There were also women who went into trances and claimed to speak directly from the gods. They were called seeresses and travelled the country with women companions, prophesying.

Burial customs

Many of the ornaments and objects which have survived from the Viking period were found by archaeologists in burial grounds. The Norsemen believed the dead had to take their riches with them into the next world, so they were buried with their treasure.

There were many different types of burial. Some were buried in coffins with mounds of earth piled over them, some in graves marked by stones in the shape of a ship and others in the buried ship itself. The body was

This gold shoulder clasp is from a burial ground at Sutton Hoo, England. It dates from before AD 700 but is typical of the treasures found in Viking sites.

sometimes cremated and sometimes not. It is even thought that some people were placed on a ship which was then set alight and floated out to sea. The dead person's horse was sometimes sacrificed and a slave girl was often killed to accompany a noble after death.

Life after death

Brave warriors who died in battle were promised their reward in the halls of the gods after death. Others do not seem to have had much to look forward to. Those who died of sickness or old age went to the Land of the Dead and suffered a gloomy fate (see page 73).

NINE WORLDS

The world of the Norse gods was arranged on three levels, one above the other. The whole was made up of nine areas, or worlds. Here you can see the Nine Worlds and the huge World-Tree, **Yggdrasil**, that grew above them and supported them. See how the world began on pages 74-75.

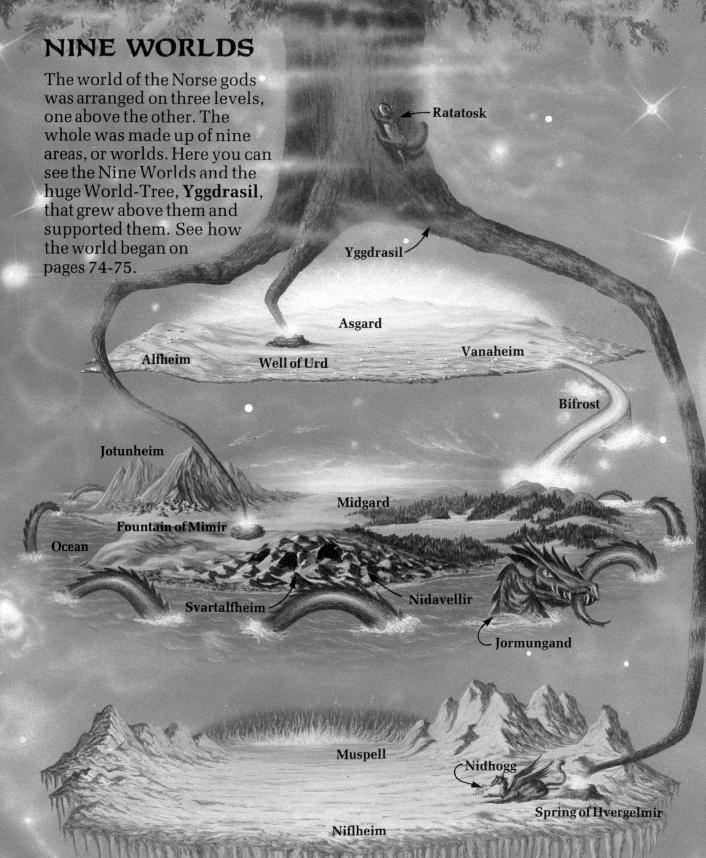

Ratatosk

Yggdrasil

Asgard

Alfheim

Well of Urd

Vanaheim

Bifrost

Jotunheim

Midgard

Fountain of Mimir

Ocean

Nidavellir

Svartalfheim

Jormungand

Muspell

Nidhogg

Spring of Hvergelmir

Niflheim

The Nine Worlds of the Norsemen

The Nine Worlds were **Asgard**, **Vanaheim** and **Alfheim** on the highest level; **Midgard**, **Jotunheim**, **Nidavellir** and **Svartalfheim** on the middle level; **Niflheim**, or **Hel** and **Muspell** on the lowest level. You can find out a bit about each of them below.

Yggdrasil

The giant ash-tree, Yggdrasil, towered above the Nine Worlds and held them firmly in place. It had three huge roots. Each root plunged into one of the levels below.

One root went into the **Spring of Hvergelmir** in Niflheim. A vile dragon called **Nidhogg** guarded the spring and gnawed at the root, trying to destroy it.

The second went into the **Fountain of Mimir** in Midgard. The water in this fountain was the source of all wisdom. It was jealously watched by the god, **Mimir** (see pages 86-87).

The third root reached into the **Well of Urd**, in Asgard, which was tended by the **Norns** . There were three Norns. They were very wise old women who tended Yggdrasil. They decided every person's destiny. Even the gods were subject to the fates they decreed.

An eagle and a hawk perched in Yggdrasil's highest branches. Deer nibbled its leaves. The squirrel, **Ratatosk**, ran up and down its trunk, carrying insults between the eagle and Nidhogg.

The leaves of the tree dripped a sweet dew that the bees used to make honey.

Asgard and Vanaheim

On the highest level were the worlds of the gods and goddesses. There were two types of god. The **Aesir** were warrior gods. They lived in Asgard. The **Vanir**, or fertility gods, lived in Vanaheim. Each deity had a magnificent hall of his or her own. A rainbow bridge, called

Bifrost, connected Asgard to Midgard, below. The watchman of this bridge was the god, **Heimdall**.

Alfheim was also on this level. It was where the **Light Elves** lived.

Midgard

Below Asgard was the Earth, or Midgard. This was the world of humans.

The **Giants** lived on this level, too. Some said their stronghold, **Utgard**, was in the barren mountains of Jotunheim far to the East. Others said that it lay across the vast **Ocean** that surrounded the Earth.

To the north of Midgard was Nidavellir. It was an area of caves and holes belonging to the **Dwarfs**. Nearby was Svartalfheim, where the troublesome **Dark Elves** lived.

Midgard was surrounded by the Ocean. It was so wide that it was thought to be impossible for humans to cross. In the Ocean lurked the terrible World-Serpent, **Jormungand**. He was so big that his body circled Midgard and took his own tail in his mouth. You can read more about him on pages 80-81 and 95.

The Land of the Dead

On the lowest level was Niflheim, the Land of the Dead. It was a gloomy place of ice, snow and eternal darkness. It was ruled by **Hel**, the gruesome Queen of the Dead (see page 81). To reach Niflheim you had to travel for nine days northwards and downwards from Midgard. At the gate waited the ghastly dog, **Garm**, with his bloodstained breast.

The fires of Muspell burned on this level, too. Muspell was guarded by **Surt** and his flaming sword. He was waiting to lead the fiery creatures of Muspell against the gods when the time of their Doom came (see page 102).

THE CREATION

The Norsemen, like all peoples, tried to explain how the world began. Here is what they believed.

Ginnungagap

Before the world existed there was a place of ice and snow in the North, called **Niflheim**. The South was an area of flames and fire named **Muspell**. Between them was a great emptiness known as **Ginnungagap**.

Ymir and Audumla

Eleven rivers flowed out of Niflheim into Ginnungagap where they froze and filled the emptiness. When the ice spread near enough to the heat of Muspell it began to melt. From the melting drops two creatures were formed. One was the first Frost Giant, **Ymir**, and the other was a huge cow, called **Audumla**. Ymir lived by drinking Audumla's milk and the cow licked the salty ice for nourishment.

While Ymir slept he sweated. From his sweat came more Frost Giants.

The birth of the gods

As Audumla was licking the ice one day, a huge, manlike shape began to appear. Within three days she licked the figure free of the ice. This was **Buri**, who in time had a son called **Bor**. Bor married **Bestla**, a Frost Giantess, and they had three sons, **Odin, Vili** and **Ve**. These became the first gods.

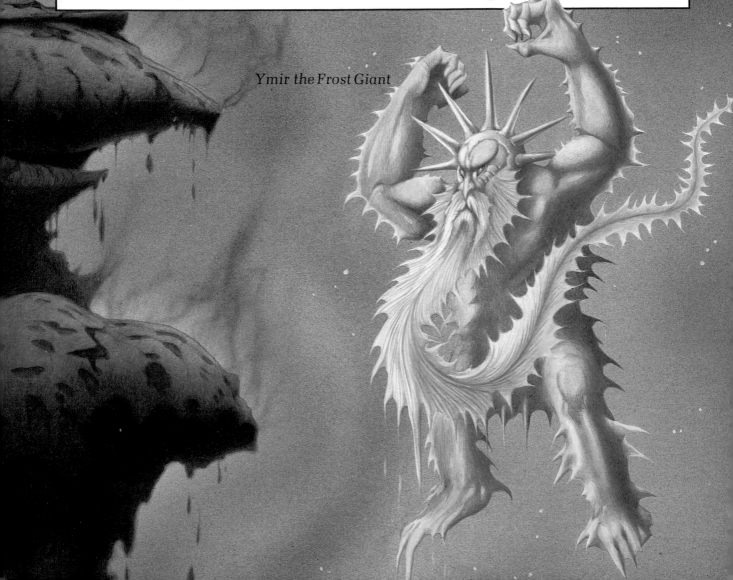

Ymir the Frost Giant

The death of Ymir

Ymir and the Frost Giants were brutal and evil. Odin and his brothers hated them. When they could not stand Ymir any more, they killed him. His blood flowed out in torrents, sweeping away all the Frost Giants except one called **Bergelmir** and his wife, who escaped in a hollow tree-trunk. All the Giants are descended from this pair.

The gods make the world

Odin, Vili and Ve dragged Ymir's body into Ginnungagap and used it to form the world. The Earth was made from his flesh. His bones and teeth became mountains and rocks and his blood filled the rivers and seas. His skull made the dome of the sky and his brains were tossed in the air as clouds.

The gods then took sparks from Muspell and threw them into the sky to be the moon, sun and stars.

The first humans

One day, while walking by the sea, Odin, Vili and Ve found the roots of an ash and an elm tree and made the first humans from them. The ash root became the first man, **Ask**, and the elm root his wife, **Embla**.

The Dwarfs

The gods noticed that maggots had appeared from Ymir's flesh and were crawling about on the Earth. They changed the maggots into small, human-shaped creatures and these became the **Dwarfs**. Four Dwarfs, called **North, South, East** and **West** were given the task of holding up the sky.

Night and Day

Night was a Giant's daughter, and **Day** was her son. Odin gave them both horse-drawn chariots and set them to drive round the world every 24 hours.

The story of Moon and Sun

A human called **Mundulfari** had a son and a daughter who were so beautiful that he called them **Moon** and **Sun** after the planets the gods had made. The gods thought this presumptuous and took the children away. They made Moon drive a chariot drawing the moon while Sun guided the sun's chariot.

Sun followed Moon across the sky. They travelled very fast because both were being chased by great wolves, who would swallow and destroy them if they caught up with them. **Skoll** was the wolf that chased Sun and the beast that pursued Moon was called **Hati**. They were the monstrous children of an ancient Giantess who lived in the Iron Wood on Earth. They eventually played a part in the gods' downfall, as you can see on page 102.

ODIN AND FRIGG

Odin was one of the Aesir, or warrior gods. He was the first god to exist, and was father of all the other gods. (His brothers, Vili and Ve, seem to fade out of Norse Mythology and it is not known what became of them.)

Odin was also King of the gods, both Aesir and Vanir. He made the Earth and sky. He created humans and all living creatures (see page 75) and ruled over them.

He was a stern and awesome king. Gods and humans feared his anger, which was not always justified. He could be spiteful and sometimes used his powers in unworthy ways (see the story of Thor and the ferryman on page 79). He was respected more than loved and was worshipped by kings and nobles rather than by ordinary people.

God of battle

As the god of battle, Odin caused wars on Earth by flinging down his spear. He decided who won, so warriors did their best to appease him. He was unpredictable, though, and did not always give victory where expected.

God of poetry and wisdom

However, Odin inspired poets as well as warriors. He made a dangerous journey to Jotunheim to obtain the Mead of Poetry (see page 97). Sometimes he allowed a human a sip of it and that person became a great poet.

He also sought very hard for wisdom and paid dearly for his knowledge (see page 87). For this reason he was worshipped by seers and magicians.

God of the dead

The bravest of the warriors slain in battle were chosen to join Odin in his great hall, Valhalla (see right). He was a god of the dead but he shared this task with others. Freyja (see page 84) entertained dead warriors. Hel (see pages 73 and 80) took those who died in their beds or of disease.

Valhalla and Valaskjalf

Valhalla, or Hall of the Slain, was Odin's magnificent hall in Asgard. Here, he sported and drank with the chosen heroes. They spent their days fighting and were revived every evening to feast and make merry.

Valhalla's walls were made of golden spears and its roof of gold shields. It had 540 doors, each big enough to let 800 armed men through, side by side.

Valaskjalf (meaning Shelf of the Slain) was Odin's other hall where his great throne, Hlidskjalf, stood. From his throne, Odin watched over the Nine Worlds. He was helped by two ravens. They flew through the Worlds gathering news which they then whispered in Odin's ears. The ravens were called Huginn (Thought) and Muninn (Memory).

The Valkyries

The Valkyries were female warriors who did Odin's will. They had frightening names like Shaker, Raging Warrior and Shrieking. They swooped over battlefields on horseback, directing the fighting. They picked the heroes to fill Valhalla. A man chosen to die was said to see a Valkyrie just before the fatal blow.

The Valkyries also worked as Odin's servants. They served food and drink to the warriors in Valhalla.

Odin's travels

Odin would often visit the other Worlds in disguise. He travelled in a blue cloak and a broad-brimmed hat which hid his face. On long journeys he rode his wonderful, eight-legged horse, Sleipnir (see page 87). His magic spear, called Gungnir, and gold arm-ring always accompanied him.

Frigg, queen of the gods

Frigg was Odin's wife and Queen of the gods. She was a Mother goddess and cared for all humans, though she was especially concerned for women and children.

Frigg and Odin had a son, called **Balder**. He died tragically (see page 101) and Frigg mourned him terribly. Because of this, many women felt she would be sympathetic to their sorrows. Their other son, **Bragi**, was married to **Idunn** (see page 89).

Although she was very beautiful and was desired by many men, she was faithful to Odin. She was a match for Odin, though, and could outwit him if she was determined to get her own way.

Like Odin, Frigg could see what the future held for any human and what their fate would be. But she would never tell what she knew.

Odin and Frigg

THOR AND SIF

Thor the Thunder-god was **Odin**'s eldest son. His mother was usually said to be **Jorth** (which means Earth). She may have been one of Odin's lovers, or Jorth could simply be a nickname for **Frigg**, who was closely linked with the Earth.

What Thor was like

Thor was an exaggerated, colourful character. He was huge, even for a god, and incredibly strong. He had wild hair and beard and a temper to match. He was never angry for long, though, and easily forgave people.

He did everything on a grand scale – feasting, drinking and fighting. He liked nothing better than a straightforward battle of strength and rarely used tricks or magic like some of the other gods.

Thor the thunder god

His brain did not always match the strength of his body and the other gods sometimes teased him for it. But people like ordinary farmers loved him for his simple outlook. He was probably the most popular of the Norse gods. His symbol was the oak tree.

Thor was called Defender of **Asgard** since he protected it from the gods' enemies. His greatest adversaries were the Giants and there are many tales of his fights with them (on page 92, for example).

God of law and order

Although Thor was a warrior he was also god of law and order, unlike Odin, who stood for war and destruction. As Thor defended Asgard against Giants, so he protected the Norsemen's homes and farms.

Thor was the Keeper of Oaths, too. Copies of his arm-ring were kept in his temples and people swore oaths on them. They were then responsible to Thor to keep their word.

Thor the thunderer

Thor raced across the sky in his chariot drawn by two giant goats, **Toothgnasher** and **Toothgrinder**. It was their hooves that people heard when it thundered on Earth. He controlled the thunder and lightning and brewed up storms by blowing through his beard. Sailors prayed to him for protection from bad weather.

Thor's magic weapons

Thor had a belt which doubled his strength when he buckled it on and iron gauntlets which allowed him to grasp any weapon. You can read about how he got them on page 91. The most famous of Thor's weapons was his hammer, **Mjollnir**. It always hit its target and returned to Thor's hands after use. When a thunderbolt struck Earth, people said that Thor had flung down his hammer.
Mjollnir did not only do harm, though. It also had protective powers and people wore small copies of it as jewellery to keep them safe and

bring good luck. These charms were used to bless the dead, newborn babies and brides. On page 93, you will see how this tradition helped Thor retrieve his hammer when it was stolen.

Thor and the ferryman

Thor was always more popular than Odin. This story helps to explain why.

Odin was annoyed with Thor. He wanted a magic horse that Thor had. Thor gave it to his son, instead of offering it to Odin (you can read about this on page 92).

Later, Thor was trudging wearily home after a hard fight against the Trolls, when he came to a swollen river. It was too deep to wade. Thor found a ferryman and asked him for a ride.

The ferryman said his name was **Harbard**. He soon proved most unpleasant. He would not take Thor on board and told him that his mother was dead and his wife had run off with a mortal. Then he began to poke fun at the god, who lost his temper and began to shout. He yelled and boasted about his brave deeds but each time the ferryman had a better story.

Thor realized the ferryman did not mean to take him across and stormed off. He had to walk miles to a ford.

Back in Asgard, he found his mother well and his wife faithful as ever. He never discovered that Harbard was Odin in disguise. This was how Odin took out his spite over the horse.

Sif

Thor was married to **Sif**, who was famous for her pure gold, flowing hair. She was a goddess of fruitfulness and plenty. Her hair reminded people of a field of ripe corn and the harvest.

In one of the myths her hair was cut and stolen (see page 90). Her misery until the hair was replaced represented the darkness of the winter season, when the corn did not grow.

Sif and Thor lived in a great hall in Asgard, called **Bilskirnir**, which means Lightning.

BALDER AND TYR

Balder was loved by everyone. He was an **Aesir** god and the son of **Odin** and **Frigg**. He was fair-haired and handsome. His face glowed and he was god of light, purity and beauty. Always gentle and kind, he was also very wise. His good judgement was sought in disputes and he was often able to reconcile enemies. He brought joy and harmony wherever he went.

Balder was happily married to **Nanna** and they lived peacefully in their hall, **Breidablik**, set in tranquil countryside in **Asgard**. They had a son, **Forseti**, who was god of justice.

Tragically, Balder's happiness was not to last. The envy and spite of **Loki** (see opposite) brought about his premature death. You can read the fatal tale and about its terrible consequences on pages 101-102.

Tyr

Tyr was the bravest of the gods. He earned his reputation through his courage in dealing with the monstrous wolf, **Fenrir** (see the story on page 88). One of his hands was torn off by Fenrir's giant jaws and he was often called the One-Handed afterwards.

Tyr was renowned for his honour. He never broke his word so, like **Thor**, he was a god of law and order. His name was used to guarantee contracts, promises and pledges. He was patron of the local gatherings (called the Thing) where Norsemen traditionally passed laws and settled disputes.

Loki's daughter Hel

LOKI

Loki had a special place among the gods. His parents were two Fire-Giants, **Farbauti** and **Laufey**, so he was not really a god. But he was the sworn brother and friend of **Odin** and lived with the **Aesir** in **Asgard**.

He was an attractive character – handsome, agile and a great joker. He loved adventures and was exciting to be with. He was nosy, inventive and loved gambling.

These attributes got him into frequent trouble, but he was wily enough to get out of most fixes. He amused the other gods but teased and exasperated them, too. He was very persuasive and the gods often took his advice, which was not always good, and got them into trouble. Only one god, **Heimdall** (see page 82) was always suspicious of Loki.

Loki was especially talented at shape-changing. He could become any animal at will. He often made mischief as a fly (see page 90) and took the form of a mare to get himself out of trouble over a bargain he and the gods made with a stranger (see page 86).

However, as time went on, it gradually became clear to the gods that Loki was not just a handsome joker. He could be cunning, deceitful and unstable. At times he told hurtful stories about others.

Eventually, the gods became wary of his behaviour and began to feel he deserved the trouble he got into when he fooled around with Giants and Dwarfs. They even began to laugh at him and take sides against him. This made Loki bitter and slowly his nature grew darker and more truly evil.

In the end, his spiteful tricks caused the death of **Balder**, which triggered **Ragnarok** or the Doom of the gods (see page 102).

Loki's brood

Odin warned Loki to have nothing to do with the Giantess, **Angrboda**, but Loki defied him and took her as his mistress. They had three monstrous children. They were the wolf, **Fenrir**; the serpent **Jormungand** who was fated to destroy **Thor** (see pages 95 and 102); and a daughter, **Hel**. Hel was grotesque. Her top half was a beautiful woman, but below the waist she was rotting and hideous, like a corpse. She became Queen of the Dead in **Niflheim**. You can read more about Loki's brood on page 88.

Sigyn, Vali and Narvi

Loki's wife was called **Sigyn**. Despite his faults, she loved him and was faithful to him. She stood by him and protected him even after he had caused Balder's death (page 101).

Sigyn and Loki had two sons, **Vali** and **Narvi**, who came to a tragic end after the death of Balder. The gods turned Vali into a wolf and he tore his brother to pieces. They then used Narvi's entrails to bind Loki for his punishment (see page 102).

NJORD, AEGIR AND HEIMDALL

Njord was the most important of the **Vanir** gods, and the chief god of fertility.

Njord was god of the sea and was therefore very important to the seafaring Vikings. He ruled the winds and waves, provided fish for fishermen and favourable winds for traders.

He lived in a hall by the sea. It was called **Noatun**, meaning Shipyard or Anchorage.

Njord married a Giantess called **Skadi**. You can read how this came about on page 89. Skadi was a great huntress and travelled miles on her snow shoes in winter with her bow and arrows.

The marriage was not a success. Skadi loved the mountains and could not bear the sea; Njord could not survive without the smell of the sea and hated the rugged mountains. In the end they lived apart.

Njord was one of the important leaders who swapped places in **Asgard** and **Vanaheim** after the war between the gods (page 86).

Aegir

Aegir and his wife, **Ran,** were also sea gods. They lived on the sea-bed and had nine daughters who moved the waves. Their personalities were changeable, like the sea they lived in. They could be pleasant or violently destructive.

They needed subjects for their kingdom so if a person fell overboard or a ship sank, they would drag the victim to the ocean floor in their nets. There, Aegir and Ran entertained them in their hall, which was crammed with treasure from shipwrecks.

Heimdall

The god **Heimdall** had some very special attributes. He was said to be the son of nine maidens. They may have been the nine daughters of Aegir and Ran . His senses were supernaturally good. He had hearing so acute that he could hear the grass grow and sight so sharp that he could detect movement a hundred miles away. He needed little sleep and was very strong.

Because of his special gifts, he was made watchman of the gods. He guarded **Bifrost**, the rainbow bridge between **Asgard** and **Midgard**. He challenged all strangers and warned the gods of their approach. He had a horn called **Gjall** which he blew in warning. It was kept by

the **Fountain of Mimir** (see page 73). Its blast sounded through the Nine Worlds at the end of the world, or **Ragnarok** (see page 102). Heimdall was **Loki's** implacable enemy. They were both fire gods and clashed all the time.

Heimdall rode a gold-maned stallion called **Gulltop**.

Heimdall's journey or the Song of Rig

Once, Heimdall paid a visit to Earth. He disguised himself as a man called **Rig**. On his journey, he came to a turf hut owned by a poor couple called **Ai** and **Edda** and asked them for food and shelter. Despite being so poor, they shared all they had with him for three nights. As a reward he caused Edda to have a son. The couple called him **Thrall** and he was ancestor to all the serfs in the world. (Serfs were poor farm workers who had no land.)

Rig next came to a comfortable farm owned by **Afi** and his wife, **Amma**. They were prosperous and gladly gave Rig shelter for three days. They were also granted a son for their kindness. He was called **Karl** and all farm-owners were descended from him. Rig moved on until he came to a gracious hall, owned by the noble **Fathir** and his wife **Mothir**. They spared no expense to entertain him for three days. Mothir, too, produced a son who was named **Jarl**.

Jarl grew up handsome and strong. One day he was out hunting when Heimdall appeared. The god taught Jarl some of the wisdom and secret knowledge of the gods. Lastly, he revealed that it was he who had caused Jarl to be born. He told the boy it was his right to go out and win land and treasures. Jarl did as he was told and became a wealthy nobleman. He married **Enna**, a chief's daughter. Their children founded the race of nobles.

Aegir and Ran

FREYJA

The most famous of all the goddesses was **Freyja**. She was a **Vanir**, daughter of the most important Vanir god, **Njord** (see page 82). She had a brother called **Freyr** (see next page). It was said that their mother was Njord's sister.

Goddess of love and beauty

Freyja was goddess of love and beauty. She had been married to the god, **Od**. He had left her and disappeared for some unknown reason. She mourned for him and when she cried she wept golden tears.

Nevertheless, she was very lovely and had many suitors. She took lovers among gods and men but spurned Giants who did not attract her, though they often wooed her.

Her love of beautiful objects sometimes overcame her good sense. Once, she lowered herself to spend the night with four Dwarfs in return for the magnificent necklace, called **Brisingamen**, that they had made.

Goddess of death

As punishment for her bad behaviour over Brisingamen, **Odin** made Freyja a goddess of death. She presided over battles and caused wars between kings on Earth. She flew over the battlefield in her chariot pulled by two cats. She chose half of the bravest warriors to accompany her to **Sessrumnir**, her hall in **Asgard**, after death.

Fertility goddess

Like all the Vanir, Freyja was a fertility goddess. She brought prosperity by granting good harvests and successful fishing. She took special care of women who were getting married or having babies and made sure many healthy children and animals were born.

The boar was her symbol, as it was her brother's. One of Freyja's nicknames was **Syr**, which means sow.

Freyja's magic

After the war between the gods (page 86) Freyja went with her father and brother to live in Asgard with the **Aesir**.

Freyja was a powerful witch and taught the Aesir her skills. She owned a magic falcon skin. When she put it on her spirit could fly through the Nine Worlds.

She made prophecies and foretold the future of all newborn babies.

FREYR

Freyja and Freyr

Freyr was the son of **Njord** (see page 82) and brother to **Freyja** (see previous page).

God of peace and plenty

As a fertility god, like his sister, Freyr granted peace and plenty to his followers. He was not a warrior god, and cared more for giving life than taking it. It was forbidden to carry arms or shed blood on land dedicated to him and outlaws were not allowed in his holy places. His worshippers prayed for his protection in battle, though, and often wore his symbol, the boar, on their helmets.

Freyr's magic possessions

Freyr owned a magic sword that moved through the air of its own accord.

He also possessed the magic ship, **Skidbladnir** (see page 90). It was big enough to hold all the gods but could be folded up and put in his pocket when not in use. It always had a favourable wind.

Freyr's chariot was pulled by a magic, golden boar called **Gullinbursti**, made by the Dwarfs (see page 90). It could run as fast as any mount.

The wooing of Gerd

Freyr was married to the Giantess, **Gerd**. This is the story of their courtship.

One day, Freyr wandered into **Odin**'s hall, **Valaskjalf**, and sat on Odin's throne. He had no right to do this. As he admired the view of the Nine Worlds his eye was drawn to **Jotunheim**, the land of the Giants.

There, leaving her father's hall, was Gerd, a dazzling Frost Giantess. Freyr fell in love on sight. But it was hopeless as he knew he would never be allowed to marry her.

Back in his own hall, Freyr despaired. He could not eat or sleep and bitterly regretted his visit to Valaskjalf. Njord grew worried. He found out what had happened from Freyr's servant, **Skirnir**. Njord was not keen to have a Frost Giantess as a daughter-in-law but could not bear to see his son suffer. So he sent Skirnir to woo Gerd for Freyr. It was too risky to let Freyr go to Jotunheim himself.

Freyr gave Skirnir his magic sword and his magic horse which could see in the dark and gallop through fire. The horse sped to Jotunheim and through the ring of icy fire round Gerd's home.

Gerd received Skirnir coldly. She rejected his offers of love, wealth and eternal youth. Like all of her kind, her heart was ice. Skirnir then tried threats. He laid Freyr's magic sword on the floor, telling Gerd that it would kill her father when he came in.

Afraid, Gerd agreed to meet Freyr. They would meet in nine days' time in the Forest of Barri. Skirnir hurried back in triumph to **Asgard**.

Freyr could hardly bear the wait, but on the ninth day he and Gerd met. Happily, the warmth of his love melted Gerd's frozen heart and she became a warm, loving creature. They returned to Asgard and lived happily there.

85

THE GODS' FIRST EXPLOITS

THE FIRST WAR

The **Vanir** gods originally had magic powers which the **Aesir** did not. **Gullveig** was a Vanir witch. She could predict the future and make gold. One day she visited the Aesir and boasted of her skills, but would not share her secrets. Infuriated, the Aesir killed her and threw her body on a fire.

She rose from the flames unharmed, however. The Aesir tried to kill her twice more but she revived each time. Finally, they were ashamed and left her alone. They gave her a new name, **Heid**, meaning gleaming one.

When the Vanir heard how Gullveig had been mistreated they were very angry. They protested and the argument turned to blows.

In the ensuing fight, the Vanir destroyed **Asgard's** walls and the Aesir did equal damage to **Vanaheim** but neither side could claim a victory so they declared a truce.

The gods decided to swap leaders as a sign of peace. Three of the greatest Vanir— **Njord**, **Freyr** and **Freyja** (see pages 82-85) – joined the Aesir. Only two Aesir went to Vanaheim in return and it was soon clear that they were not of the same quality. These were the warrior, **Honir** and **Mimir**, guardian of the Fountain of Knowledge.

Honir was very brave and Mimir was extremely wise so the Vanir welcomed them at first. But although they worked well together, Honir on his own became confused and could not make intelligent decisions.

The Vanir felt cheated and in revenge they chopped off Mimir's head and sent it back to **Odin**. He preserved it with magic herbs and gave it the power of speech so it could still pass on Mimir's wisdom. He kept it by the Fountain of Knowledge.

Despite these problems, the peace held and the Aesir learned the magic of the Vanir.

REBUILDING ASGARD'S WALL

The **Aesir** were anxious to rebuild **Asgard's** wall. It had been ruined in the war with the **Vanir** (see left). But they could not find anyone to do the job.

Then one day a rider came to Asgard, saying he had a proposal for the gods. He offered to repair the wall. His price was the moon, the sun and **Freyja** as his wife.

The gods (especially Freyja) were outraged but sly **Loki** suggested the gods should accept on condition the work was completed, without help, in six months. They knew this would be impossible, but if the builder agreed, they would get most of the wall mended without paying since the contract would be broken.

The stranger agreed to the terms as long as he could have the help of his horse, **Svadilfari**, which the gods allowed.

The horse dragged huge rocks to the wall in a net and the stranger worked so hard it began to

seem he would complete the work in time. The gods were furious and told Loki he must get them out of the bargain.

Loki, the Shape-Changer, had an idea. As the stranger took Svadilfari to fetch a final load of rocks on the last day of the six months, Loki appeared disguised as a beautiful mare and pranced around playfully. Svadilfari ran after the mare into the woods and could not be caught. The workman could not finish the job without him, so he failed.

In his fury, the builder burst out of his magic disguise, revealing his true shape as a Rock-Giant. The gods then had no qualms about killing him for trying to fool them.

Loki wisely stayed away from Asgard for a while. When he returned he brought a fantastic, eight-legged horse, called **Sleipnir**. Sleipnir was the son of Svadilfari and the mare Loki had been. He could gallop over land, sea and air. Loki gave the horse to **Odin** to regain his favour.

Loki on Sleipnir

ODIN'S WISDOM

Odin was hungry for all the wisdom in the world. He began by making a journey and asking questions of everyone he met – Elves, Dwarfs and Giants.

In **Jotunheim** Odin learnt all he could from **Mimir**, guard of the Fountain of Knowledge. Keen to know more, he asked to drink from the Fountain itself. Mimir said he could but that he must pay a high price – one of his eyes. Odin agreed and was one-eyed from then on.

Still Odin wanted to learn more. To do so he paid the final penalty. He became a

sacrificial victim. He hung from a branch of **Yggdrasil** with a spear in his side for nine days and nights. After this ordeal he died. Thus he learnt the wisdom of the dead. By his supernatural powers he came to life again and used what he had learnt for the good of gods and mortals.

Odin brought the Runes from the Land of the Dead. These were magic symbols that warded off danger. Odin taught them to mankind and they carved them in stone to provide magic protection.

THE GODS IN DANGER

THE BINDING OF FENRIR

The **Norns** warned the gods that the unnatural children of **Loki** and the evil Giantess, **Angrboda** (see page 81), could bring disaster upon them. So the gods decided to act.

They raided Angrboda's hall and seized her monstrous brood. **Odin** grabbed the serpent **Jormungand** and threw him into the **Ocean.** **Hel** (half-woman, half-corpse) was banished to **Niflheim**. The giant wolf, **Fenrir**, seemed harmless so the gods let him wander free.

These precautions were not enough, though. Jormungand terrorized the seas, Hel became feared as Queen of the Dead and Fenrir grew so fierce that the Norns warned he would cause Odin's death if something was not done.

The gods could not pollute the sacred ground of **Asgard** by simply killing Fenrir, but he had grown so powerful that it was hard to think of a way to restrain him.

Eventually they decided on a trick. They asked Fenrir to test the strength of an iron chain they had made. They tied it round him, hoping he would be unable to break it, but he escaped easily. The gods produced another, stronger chain and tried the same trick, but Fenrir snapped it without effort.

Fenrir

The gods were seriously worried. They sent **Freyr's** servant, **Skirnir**, to the Dwarfs, offering huge rewards for a chain that could bind Fenrir. He returned with what looked like a silken ribbon. The ribbon was magic, however, and was unbreakable.

Once more, they asked Fenrir to test his strength. By now Fenrir was becoming suspicious. When he saw the strange ribbon he refused to be tied in it. The gods promised to free him if the ribbon proved too strong, but Fenrir did not trust them. At last the wolf agreed to the test if one of the gods would put a hand in his mouth as a sign of good faith while he made the attempt. The gods hesitated, then **Tyr** put his hand between Fenrir's teeth.

The wolf was tied up and soon found that however he strained, the bonds got tighter. The gods refused to free him so he clashed his jaws shut and bit off Tyr's hand.

They dragged Fenrir deep underground and tied him to a rock out of harm's way. This was not the end of Angrboda's children, though, as you will find out on page 102.

IDUNN AND THE GOLDEN APPLES

Odin, Loki and **Honir** went exploring on Earth. When they got hungry Loki killed an ox while the others lit a fire. They set the meat to roast but, strangely, it would not cook.

Then the gods heard a voice. It was an eagle in the tree above. He claimed he was preventing the meat from cooking. He would remove his spell if the gods let him eat his fill. The hungry gods agreed and the eagle at once snatched all the best bits.

Loki was enraged and attacked the eagle with a staff. The bird grabbed the staff and flew off with Loki still dangling from it. Loki tried to let go but was held by magic. The eagle deliberately dragged Loki over thorn bushes, glaciers and rocks until he promised he would do anything if the eagle would only let him go.

Loki was made to promise to lure the goddess **Idunn** and her golden apples out of **Asgard** sometime in the next seven days. The golden apples were magic fruit which kept the gods young. Idunn was their keeper.

Loki tricked Idunn into leaving Asgard with her apples. He told her he had found a tree in **Midgard** that bore golden fruit. It might be a new source of the precious apples. He persuaded her to investigate, taking her apples for comparison.

As soon as Idunn set foot in Midgard the eagle swooped down and carried her off to **Jotunheim**. For he was really the Giant **Thiazi** in disguise.

Without the apples, the gods grew old and feeble. They did not know where Idunn was and could not think what to do. **Heimdall** said he had seen Idunn leave Asgard with Loki. They questioned Loki until he told them the truth. They then threatened to kill him unless he brought her back.

Freyja lent Loki her magic falcon skin and he flew to Thiazi's stronghold. He found Idunn a prisoner there. He turned her into a nut so he could carry her in his beak, then fled back to Asgard. Thiazi saw her escape and gave chase in his eagle disguise.

The gods had lit fires to guide Loki and he flew safely over the walls of Asgard. Thiazi plunged after him but in his haste he singed his wings and fell to earth. The gods soon finished him off, despite their weak, aged state. Loki restored Idunn to her proper shape and her golden apples soon revived the gods.

Thiazi's daughter, **Skadi**, came to Asgard seeking compensation for her father's death. The gods offered her one of themselves as a husband but they said she must choose from their feet only. She picked the shapeliest pair, hoping they were **Balder's**. They proved to be **Njord's**, which did not please Skadi (see page 82 for more about their marriage). She was appeased in the end when Odin placed her father's eyes in the sky as stars and gave her the gift of laughter to cheer her up.

MAGIC GIFTS FOR THE GODS

TREASURES OF THE GODS

Once when **Thor** was off fighting Giants, **Loki** crept into **Sif's** bedroom and cut off all her wonderful, golden hair.

Thor returned to find Sif heartbroken. He threatened to break every bone in Loki's body unless he replaced her hair.

Loki went to the Dwarfs for help. They made a magic length of hair from spun gold that grew like real hair.

At the same time, they made a magic ship, **Skidbladnir**, and a spear called **Gungnir**. They gave them to Loki for the gods, hoping to win their gratitude.

Loki took the gifts and, on his way home, he visited two more Dwarfs, **Brokk** and **Eitri**. Craftily hoping to get more treasures, he bet his own head that they could not make gifts to equal those he already had.

Challenged, the two Dwarfs forged a golden boar, a gold arm-ring and a war hammer.

Pleased with himself, Loki hurried back to **Asgard**, where he gave Sif her hair. Then he offered **Odin** the arm-ring. He gave **Freyr** the ship and the boar, **Gullinbursti**. He presented the hammer to Thor . It was called **Mjollnir**.

Then Brokk turned up to ask if the gods liked his work. They agreed it was as good as the rest, so he demanded Loki's head in payment of their bet.

What Brokk did not know was that while he had been forging his gifts, Loki had turned into a fly and distracted him just long enough to make him forge Mjollnir's handle slightly too short for perfection. Loki now pointed this out but the gods thought it was a shabby trick and that he deserved to lose his head.

Loki's last chance was a trick with words. He agreed that the Dwarf could have his head, but must not take any of his neck. It was not possible to take one without touching the other, so Loki was saved. Brokk contented

himself with sewing up Loki's mouth to teach him a lesson. The gods laughed at Loki.

Loki went off alone and ripped out the painful stitches. He felt humiliated and resented the gods' laughter. From this time he began to plot his revenge.

The Dwarfs at work

THOR'S MAGIC BELT AND GLOVES

Loki was wearing **Freyja's** falcon skin when the evil Giant, **Geirrod**, caught him. Geirrod and his two foul daughters saw the strange glitter in the bird's eyes and realized it must be a god or magician in disguise.

Loki refused to admit who he was, so Geirrod shut him in a box without food until he gave in. Geirrod said he would be released if he promised to bring **Thor**, unarmed, to the Giant's hall. Loki agreed.

Thor simply enjoyed Loki's company so when he proposed a trip to **Midgard** to meet "two lovely girls", Thor happily went along. Since it was meant to be a pleasure-trip, he left **Mjollnir** at home.

On the way, the gods stayed with the friendly Giantess, **Grid**. Thor mentioned that they were going to meet Geirrod's daughters. Later, when Loki was asleep, Grid explained to Thor that Geirrod was an enemy and was probably plotting something. She gave Thor a belt, which doubled his strength, some iron gauntlets and a magic staff. Loki was worried when he saw Thor's new equipment but dared not say anything.

Next day they came to a river of blood which they tried to wade, but the flow grew deeper and faster. Thor then saw a hideous Giantess who was sending the blood in waves towards them. This was one of Geirrod's daughters. He threw a rock to drive her off but still had to clutch Loki and grab hold of a branch to avoid being swept away.

When they reached Geirrod's hall no one was there so Thor sat down and dozed off. He woke to find his chair being lifted to the ceiling by Geirrod's daughters, who intended to crush him against the roof.

Thor used Grid's staff to push himself away from the beams, then he killed the evil Giantesses. Geirrod himself appeared next, with a ball of red-hot iron held in tongs. He threw it at Thor, who caught it in his iron gloves. He hurled it back with all the strength lent him by Grid's belt. The Giant was killed and Thor returned safely to Asgard. He never really trusted Loki again, though.

THOR AND THE GIANTS

The Giant Hrungnir

THOR'S HEADACHE

One day **Odin** went looking for adventure in **Jotunheim** on his fantastic horse, **Sleipnir**.

The Giant **Hrungnir** saw him coming and was very impressed by Sleipnir. He challenged Odin to a race against his own horse, **Gullfaxi**. Odin accepted.

The horses were a good match and Hrungnir was so busy racing that he did not realize they were heading straight for **Asgard**. They were over the wall into the home of the gods before he knew it.

Hrungnir was sure he had been led into a trap, but Odin seemed friendly and offered him a drink. The gods were scandalized to see a Giant in Asgard. Odin warned them not to harm an unarmed guest.

Hrungnir began to relax and enjoy himself. He drank as much as the **Valkyries** could bring him and became very drunk and rowdy.

Odin began to feel that the Giant was getting out of hand. He sent for **Thor**, who was indignant at Hrungnir's behaviour, and would have dealt swiftly with him. But Hrungnir was quick to point out that it would be cowardly for Thor to kill him as he had no weapon. Thor restrained himself, but arranged to meet Hrungnir in single combat at another time.

The day of the duel came and the enemies faced each other. Thor hurled **Mjollnir** at the Giant. Hrungnir held up a huge whetstone, which he used to sharpen his tools, as a shield.

The hammer shattered the whetstone and one of the sharp, flying chips entered Thor's head. He fell, wounded. But Mjollnir reached its mark, despite the whetstone shield, and Hrungnir was killed. He fell dead on top of Thor. The gods tried to pull Thor from under the Giant but could not shift him.

Thor ordered his servant, **Thialfi**, to go to the Giantess, **Jarnsaxa**. She was an ally of the gods and she and Thor had a son called **Magni**. He was only three years old but already had the combined strength of his parents.

Magni freed Thor easily. Thor was delighted with his son and gave him Hrungnir's horse, Gullfaxi, in thanks. This offended Odin, who had fancied the horse for himself. Odin made Thor pay for this later (see page 79).

From then on, the chip of whetstone in Thor's head gave him terrible headaches.

THE THEFT OF THOR'S HAMMER

Thor woke one morning to find his hammer gone. The worried gods held a council to decide what to do.

Loki offered to find the hammer and **Freyja** lent him her falcon skin so he could fly swiftly in search of it.

He soon discovered that it was **Thrym**, a Frost Giant, who had **Mjollnir**. Thrym said he would return it only if he was sent Freyja as his wife.

Freyja shook with indignation and shed gold tears. This amused Loki who encouraged the gods to send her to Thrym. But **Heimdall**, who disliked Loki, came up with a plan.

Heimdall's plan was that Thor should dress up as a bride and pretend to be Freyja. Once in Thrym's hall he could perhaps recover his hammer. Loki went along to join in the fun, disguised as a bridesmaid.

When Thor and Loki arrived at Thrym's hall the wedding feast was laid. Thor nearly gave himself away by his outrageous appetite, but Loki explained it by saying the "bride" had not eaten for days in her excitement.

Delighted that she was so eager, Thrym called for Mjollnir to bless the bride. He placed the hammer on her knees in the traditional way. At once, Thor grabbed it and threw off his veil. The Giants ran for their lives, though Thor killed Thrym and several others.

93

THOR'S LESSON IN UTGARD

Thor and **Loki** went to visit **Utgard**. On their way they stayed with a couple so poor that they only had vegetable soup to offer the gods. So Thor killed the goats that pulled his chariot and they had a feast. Thor saved the goats' skins and insisted that all the bones be kept.

The couple's son, **Thialfi**, loved marrow and secretly snapped one of the goats' thighbones to suck. He hid the broken bone under the rest.

Next day, Thor waved his hammer over the skins and bones and brought the goats back to life. But one of them was lame and Thialfi had to confess. Thor took him and his sister, **Roskva**, along as servants in repayment.

One night they discovered a strange hall in the forest. Its door filled the width of one wall. Inside they found a small room off the main hall and slept there. In the night they were woken by a roaring and the ground shook. They were uneasy and left at dawn.

Outside they found the source of the disturbance. It was a Giant snoring. The "hall" was his glove and they had slept in its thumb. The Giant woke and introduced himself as **Skrymir**. He offered to guide them to Utgard and took their food bag to carry. He strode on ahead. When they caught up he was asleep and had sealed the food bag by magic so they could not get anything to eat.

That night Skrymir kept them all awake with his snoring again. Unable to bear it, Thor rose and bashed him over the head with **Mjollnir**. Skrymir went on snoring loudly. Thor hit him three more times but the Giant simply woke complaining that an acorn must have dropped on his head.

Skrymir walked ahead again the next day. He said he would prepare a welcome for them but they found the gates of Utgard closed and had to squeeze through the bars.

At last they reached the hall of the Giant King, **Utgard-Loki**. He laughed at Thor's group and called them puny. He challenged them to beat the Giants at anything.

Loki offered to out-eat anyone. A huge meal was laid and he and the Giant, **Logi**, started to gobble. They met in the middle of the table. Loki ate all his food but Logi chewed bones and dishes, too, so he won.

Thialfi agreed to a race. He ran his fastest but his Giant opponent finished before Thialfi had got half-way.

Thor was sure he could drink more than anyone else. Utgard-Loki gave him a huge drinking horn. He put it to his lips but could not drain it however he gulped.

The Giants then set Thor some easier tasks. First, to lift the King's cat, but he could hardly heave one paw off the ground. Then, to wrestle with an old woman, the King's foster-mother, who got Thor down on one knee.

Humbled and ashamed, Thor let Utgard-Loki show him to the gates of Utgard. There, the King said that now Thor was safely out of Utgard he would confess to tricking him.

Utgard-Loki admitted that Skrymir had been himself in disguise. When Thor had struck him his head had been protected by a magic, invisible hill. He showed Thor the hill and the deep valleys made by his blows.

The Giant whom Loki had challenged was really Fire, which eats everything in its path.

Thialfi had run against Thought, the fastest-moving thing in the world.

Thor's drinking horn had had its tip in the Ocean, which was impossible to drain.

The cat was actually **Jormungand** in disguise, and the old woman was Old Age, who overcomes everyone in the end.

Utgard-Loki warned the gods never to set foot in his kingdom again. Then he and his stronghold vanished. Thor felt a terrible fool, but it had taught him a lesson.

Thor hooks Jormungand

THOR GOES FISHING

The gods ran out of drink so they went to see **Aegir**, who brewed the best ale. He did not have a pot big enough to hold ale for all the gods and asked **Thor** to get him one.

Tyr's mother was married to the Giant, **Hymir**. She would have a suitable cauldron. So Tyr and Thor went to see her. They knew Hymir disliked gods, so they went in disguise.

Tyr's mother welcomed them with a good meal. Hymir was grumpy, especially when Thor polished off two whole oxen. He moaned that now they would have to go hunting.

Next day, Thor and Hymir went fishing. The Giant caught two whales and was pleased with himself. Then Thor cast his line, baited with an ox-head. There was a great thrashing and **Jormungand** himself rose up and snatched the bait. Thor struggled with the serpent and the boat nearly capsized, but he managed to strike it on the head with **Mjollnir**. Stunned, Jormungand sank below the waves. Hymir was impressed.

Then Thor asked to borrow the cauldron. Hymir sulkily said he could if he could smash a certain glass that he produced. Thor flung it at a pillar but the glass was magic and the pillar broke. Tyr's mother told Thor how to break the spell by throwing the glass at Hymir's head. He did so and the glass smashed.

Hymir then had to hand over the cauldron.

95

TALES OF MAGIC AND DISGUISE

OTTAR'S ANCESTORS

Ottar was a handsome young prince who was devoted to **Freyja**. He built shrines and made sacrifices until Freyja had to notice him. When she saw him she fell in love and went to **Midgard** to be with him.

One thing marred their happiness. Ottar had a rival for his throne, called **Angantyr**. To decide which of them should become king without bloodshed they fixed a contest. The one who could correctly recite the longest list of his ancestors would win.

This was no easy task. The only person who knew Ottar's whole family tree was a disagreeable Giantess called **Hyndla**. She also had a magic beer which would enable him to remember all the names.

Freyja wanted to help Ottar. She turned him into her battle-boar, **Hildisvini**, and rode off to see Hyndla. Freyja did not reveal the real reason for her visit but Hyndla guessed it. The Giantess refused to help and took delight in insulting Freyja. With difficulty, Freyja kept her temper and finally persuaded Hyndla to give her the names of Ottar's ancestors.

But however Freyja cajoled, Hyndla refused to give Ottar a sip of the vital memory beer. The goddess lost patience. Tired of being nice, she threw a circle of flame round the Giantess, which drew in closer and closer. Hyndla was afraid and saved herself by giving Ottar a sip of beer, though she cursed it as he drank.

Freyja was not concerned. She could protect Ottar from any curse of Hyndla's.

HOW DENMARK GOT BIGGER

King **Gylfi** of Sweden set out to discover how his subjects were faring. He went travelling in disguise and one night he came across an old beggar-woman. She shared all she had with him – food, fire and blanket. They talked all night and Gylfi learnt a lot from her.

Next morning, Gylfi thanked the woman, then told her who he was. He offered her as much of his kingdom as she could plough with four oxen in a day and a night in return for her kindness.

The old woman was really the goddess **Gefion**. She felt that Gylfi's reward was too generous.

A real beggar-woman would have been overwhelmed to receive so much for so little. Although Gylfi had meant well, she decided to teach him a lesson.

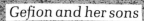

Gefion and her sons

Gefion called her four sons from **Jotunheim**. Their father was a Giant. She was goddess of ploughing and their sons had been born as giant oxen. They went to Sweden and in a day and a night they ploughed a huge chunk of land with their supernatural strength.

They dragged the ploughed land to the coast and floated it over the sea to Denmark. There, they anchored it off the coast and it became the island of Zealand. The hole left in Sweden filled with water and became Lake Malar.

THE MEAD OF POETRY

When the **Aesir** and **Vanir** made peace (see page 86) they all spat into a great jar to seal the treaty. From the divine spittle they shaped a man, called **Kvasir**. He inherited the gods' wisdom and his advice was highly valued.

Two nasty Dwarfs, **Fjalar** and **Galar**, wanted to steal Kvasir's wisdom. They asked him to a feast, then murdered him, catching his blood in two jars and a cauldron. Mixed with honey it made a heady Mead which inspired wisdom and poetry.

These Dwarfs later quarrelled with the Giant, **Gilling**, and killed him. His brother, **Suttung** came looking for him and would have killed the Dwarfs in revenge but they saved their skins by giving him the precious Mead.

Suttung dug a cavern deep in the mountains to store the Mead and set his daughter, **Gunnlod**, to guard it. He boasted about his treasure, though, and soon the gods heard of it and decided that such a precious liquid should belong to them.

Odin disguised himself as a handsome Giant named **Bolverk**. He went to the home of Suttung's brother, **Braugi**, and tricked his servants into killing each other. He then offered to help Braugi, saying he could do the work of nine men all summer. In return he asked for just one sip of the Mead of Poetry. Braugi agreed, though he was not sure Suttung would allow it.

At the end of the summer, Braugi had to admit that he could not keep the bargain. So Bolverk made him tell where the Mead was kept and bore a hole into the cavern with his magic auger, or drill. Odin at once turned into a snake and wriggled down the hole.

In the cavern, Odin became Bolverk again. He paid court to Gunnlod, who fell in love with him. Soon, he persuaded her to give him a sip of Mead. When she brought him the jars, he quickly drained all three. He held the Mead in his mouth and turned himself into an eagle to fly back to **Asgard**. And that was how the gods got the Mead of Poetry.

THE CURSE OF THE RING

ANDVARI'S GOLD

Odin, **Loki** and **Honir** were once again in **Midgard**, dressed as ordinary men. By a river they watched an otter catch a salmon. Loki killed the otter for its fine skin and they had the salmon for supper.

They asked for shelter that night at a nearby farm. The farmer, **Hreidmar**, was strangely unwelcoming but the gods put it down to bad manners and soon fell asleep.

In the night, Hreidmar and his sons, **Regin** and **Fafnir**, seized their guests and tied them up. Odin demanded an explanation and Hreidmar revealed that he was a magician. Each day he turned one of his sons into an otter to go fishing. The strangers had killed him.

The gods were shocked and offered to compensate. The farmer asked for enough gold to stuff the otter skin and make a pile over it when held upright.

Loki was freed to fetch the gold. He dived to the sea-bed to borrow **Ran's** net which caught whatever it was cast at. Then he sought out a pool deep in the caves of **Svartalfheim**. He cast the net and caught a huge pike which immediately resumed its real shape as **Andvari**, a Dwarf.

Andvari was famous for his hoard of gold. Loki threatened to strangle him unless he handed it all over. The Dwarf had no choice and led Loki to his secret store.

Loki's sack was full and he was about to leave when he spotted a gold ring on Andvari's finger. Andvari begged Loki not to take it, but he insisted. Dancing with rage, Andvari placed a curse on the gold to bring misery to whoever owned it. The ring he cursed to destroy its wearer.

When Loki returned, Odin and Honir were freed. The otter skin was stuffed with gold and held up by the tail. Gold was piled over it until it was hidden except for one whisker.

Hreidmar demanded Andvari's gold ring, which Loki had kept, to finish the job. Loki warned him of the curse, but he did not care.

Before long, the curse began to work. Greedy for the gold, Fafnir murdered his father. Regin claimed his half of the treasure but Fafnir ran off with the lot. Using the skills learnt from his father, Fafnir turned himself into a dragon and jealously guarded his trove.

Regin wandered far away but he brooded on revenge and eventually found a way to destroy Fafnir (see below).

THE CURSE IS FULFILLED

Many stories are told of how the curse on **Andvari's** gold ended. This is probably the best-known.

After **Fafnir** killed his father to get **Andvari's** gold (see above), his sister, **Hjordis,** married **Sigmund**. Sigmund died before their son, **Sigurd**, was born. Fafnir's brother, **Regin**, cared for his nephew.

Regin taught Sigurd that it was his duty to avenge his grandfather and kill Fafnir, who had become a dragon to guard his trove.

Sigurd grew up strong and brave and slew the dragon. He roasted and ate its heart, whose magic enabled him to talk to the birds.

The gold was now Regin's but he could not bear to share it, even with Sigurd, so he plotted to kill him. The birds warned Sigurd who killed Regin to save himself. He then inherited the gold.

Meanwhile, the **Valkyrie Brynhild** was in trouble. She sometimes became a swan, flew to Earth and removed her disguise to go swimming. One day, a man stole her feathers and would not return them until she had changed the course of a battle.

Brynhild's meddling brought defeat to one of **Odin's** favourites. As punishment, Odin put her into a magic sleep in a castle ringed by fire.

She would only wake if someone braved the flames. Even so, she would no longer be a Valkyrie but a human.

It was Sigurd, seeking the chance to prove his courage, who rescued Brynhild. They fell in love and planned to marry. Before the wedding could take place, Sigurd visited King **Giuki** and Queen **Grimhild** of the Nibelungs. Wicked Grimhild knew of Sigurd's gold and wanted it. She gave him a love potion so he fell in love with and married her daughter, **Gudrun**, forgetting Brynhild.

Gudrun's brother, **Gunnar**, wanted to marry Brynhild. Indifferent now, Sigurd wooed her for him. Brynhild married Gunnar but was so hurt and jealous that she arranged Sigurd's murder, then killed herself.

The curse continued. The gold now belonged entirely to the Nibelungs. Gudrun re-married and made her husband, **Alti**, kill Sigurd's murderer. Then Alti killed Gudrun's brothers so she caused his death in revenge. Gudrun herself and her sons all died violently before the curse faded.

The guardian of the gold

AGNAR AND GEIRROD

The King of the Goths had two sons called **Agnar** and **Geirrod**. When Agnar was ten and Geirrod eight they took a boat to go fishing, despite warnings never to go out alone.

A storm arose and the boys were driven far out to sea. By next morning they were near an unknown shore. The nearest shelter was a poor hut, where they were welcomed by an old peasant couple. As the winter weather had closed in, the boys could not go home and stayed there during the cold months.

The peasants treated them kindly. The old man liked Geirrod best, while his wife favoured Agnar. They both taught the boys many things. When spring came they put them in a boat and sent them home.

The peasants were actually **Odin** and **Frigg** in disguise. Geirrod was really a horrid boy, although Odin preferred him. As the brothers neared their home shore, Geirrod grabbed the oars, jumped overboard and pushed the boat back out to sea, leaving Agnar adrift.

Geirrod went home and told his father that Agnar had drowned. The king was overjoyed to see his younger son. He named Geirrod his heir and in time he became king.

Agnar survived but led a wild life. Geirrod grew up even worse and was a very bad king. He was cruel and greedy for gold.

Odin and Frigg watched their foster-sons with interest. Odin teased Frigg about Agnar's wild ways, but would not hear a word against Geirrod. Frigg was annoyed and dared Odin to go to Geirrod's court in disguise to see for himself how guests were treated.

Frigg sent her maid, **Fulla**, to warn Geirrod against a magician who might come to his court. Geirrod would know him because the dogs would not bark at him.

Soon a stranger in a blue cloak and large hat appeared at court. The fierce dogs ignored him and Geirrod thought this must be the very magician. The visitor gave his name as **Grimnir**, but instead of being welcomed he was tied to a spit between two fires.

Only Geirrod's son, called **Agnar** after his lost uncle, took pity on Grimnir. He brought him a horn of ale to ease his suffering. Suddenly, Odin threw off his disguise and broke his bonds. Terrified, Geirrod tried to attack him but fell on his own sword and was killed. Odin vanished, but watched over young Agnar when he became king as a reward for his kindness.

THE DEATH OF BALDER

Balder, the gentlest god, began to have nightmares about death. He told **Odin** and **Frigg**, but neither they nor the other gods could explain it.

Odin galloped to **Niflheim** on **Sleipnir**. In **Hel's** hall he sought out the ghost of a great seeress. She said Balder was doomed and that Odin could not prevent it.

Frigg would not accept Balder's fate. She made a list of every harmful thing, then went through the Nine Worlds making them swear never to hurt Balder. Fire, water, stones, metals, plants and birds and diseases all swore. Frigg felt happier, believing nothing could now kill her son.

The gods found a new game. They threw things at Balder just to see them turn safely aside. Only **Loki** was not happy. He was jealous of Balder. Disguised as an old woman, he questioned Frigg. She admitted that one plant had not made the promise – an insignificant sprig of mistletoe.

Full of hatred, Loki found the plant and made a dart from it. He joined the gods in their latest game and asked Balder's blind brother, **Hod**, if he would like to play. Hod was delighted. Loki gave him the mistletoe dart and guided his aim. It pierced Balder's heart and he fell dead.

Frigg begged someone to go to Niflheim and offer Hel any ransom she asked to release Balder from death. **Hermod**, one of Odin's sons, volunteered.

Balder's body was given a hero's burial. It was placed on his ship, which was piled with treasure and set alight. The Giantess **Hyrrokin** pushed it out to sea. Balder's wife, **Nanna**, died of a broken heart and was buried with him.

In Niflheim, Hermod told Hel why he had come. She said that if Balder was so well-loved, everyone and everything in the Nine Worlds would weep for him. If they did, she would let him return to **Asgard**.

Hermod hurried back with this news and the gods at once went to every corner of the Nine Worlds, asking everyone and everything to cry for Balder. But there was one evil Giantess who would not weep. No amount of pleading would make her shed a tear, so Balder had to stay in the Land of the Dead. The Giantess was actually Loki in disguise. He smiled at what he had done.

Hyrrokin with Balder's funeral ship

LOKI'S PUNISHMENT

Loki avoided the gods after **Balder's** death. The gods mourned bitterly, but eventually decided the mourning must end. So **Aegir** and **Ran** held a feast. **Thor** was away fighting Trolls and Loki was not invited but everyone else was there.

In the middle of the banquet, Loki appeared. Goaded by the sight of the gods' happiness, he began to mock them each in turn. He pointed out their weaknesses and told their secrets.

At this moment Thor came in. Loki threw insults at him, too, then fled. The gods had had enough. They set off to hunt Loki, who became a salmon and leapt into a waterfall to escape. The gods knew his tricks by now and were not fooled. They caught him in a net, which was fitting as Loki had invented the net when Ran was looking for something to catch fish in.

The gods decided that death was too easy for Loki and that he ought to suffer. They turned his son **Vali** into a wolf and let him tear his brother **Narvi** to pieces. They tied Loki across sharp rocks in a cave deep in the mountains.

Skadi placed a great snake among the stalactites hanging from the roof. It dripped venom from its fangs onto Loki's face, causing him agony. The gods felt that this torture was just, but took no joy in their revenge.

Loki's loving wife **Sigyn** sat by her husband. Whatever he had done, she forgave him. She held a bowl to catch the poison and spare Loki's pain. But now and then she had to empty the bowl and the fiery poison struck Loki once more. He writhed in agony until the Earth shook.

Loki's wickedness and **Balder's** death herald the coming of the end of the world. This is to be the Doom of the gods, called **Ragnarok**, and is still to come.

RAGNAROK

According to predictions, quarrels between gods and Giants will become fiercer and more frequent at this time. There will be constant war on Earth and men will slay their own fathers and brothers. **Midgard** will freeze, killing all humans, except one pair who will climb into **Yggdrasil's** branches for refuge.

Garm and Tyr

The dreadful wolves, **Skoll** and **Hati** (see page 75), will finally catch and swallow the sun and moon. The stars will go out, leaving the world in darkness.

Loki and **Fenrir** will break their chains and join sides against the gods. **Jormungand** will heave himself out of the waves and invade the land, making the Earth shudder.

Loki will lead an attack on **Asgard**. The Giants and the fiery beings from **Muspell** will join him. **Hel** will bring her dead souls to fight on his side with **Garm** and all evil creatures.

Heimdall's horn, **Gjall**, will sound a warning through the Nine Worlds. The field of battle has already been chosen. It is a vast plain, called **Vigard**, and there the gods will face their enemies and they will destroy each other.

Fenrir will kill **Odin** and then be killed by Odin's son, **Vidar**; Loki and Heimdall will slay each other; **Thor** will destroy Jormungand, only to die from the serpent's venom; Garm and **Tyr** will die fighting each other and thousands more will perish in the gruesome battle.

Surt (see page 73) will fling fire in all directions and destroy Asgard and Midgard. The Earth will sink into the sea and all life vanish. That is Ragnarok, the end of the world.

A NEW START

All hope for the future does not end at **Ragnarok**, however. Although the Nine Worlds will be destroyed, **Yggdrasil** will survive. Land will rise again from the **Ocean** and a fresh, green Earth will emerge. **Lif** and **Lifthrasir**, the couple who hid in Yggdrasil, will climb down and renew the human race.

Before the sun is swallowed by **Skoll**, she will have a daughter who will return after Ragnarok to light the new world. Plants and animals will gradually reappear.

There will be survivors among the gods, too. Odin's sons, **Vidar** and **Vali** are expected to remain alive. **Thor's** sons, **Modi** and **Magni** are destined to find **Mjollnir** and carry on. **Balder**, **Nanna**, **Hod** and **Honir** will revive and start a new race of gods who will live in peace.

WHO'S WHO

This section is a Who's Who of characters and creatures in the Norse Myths. Any character, place or object whose name appears in bold type in this book has an entry here. Places and Things are in their own sections on page 111.

The Who's Who tells you about the family, doings, personality, appearance and magic powers of each character. It is arranged alphabetically and some abbreviations have been used to save space. You can find out how to understand the entries in the example below.

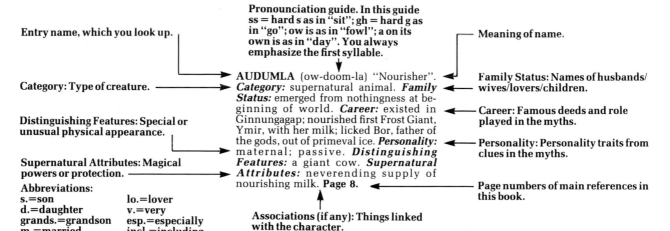

Entry name, which you look up.

Category: Type of creature.

Distinguishing Features: Special or unusual physical appearance.

Supernatural Attributes: Magical powers or protection.

Abbreviations:
s.=son
d.=daughter
grands.=grandson
m.=married
lo.=lover
v.=very
esp.=especially
incl.=including

Pronounciation guide. In this guide ss = hard s as in "sit"; gh = hard g as in "go"; ow is as in "fowl"; a on its own is as in "day". You always emphasize the first syllable.

Meaning of name.

Family Status: Names of husbands/wives/lovers/children.

Career: Famous deeds and role played in the myths.

Personality: Personality traits from clues in the myths.

Page numbers of main references in this book.

AUDUMLA (ow-doom-la) "Nourisher". *Category:* supernatural animal. *Family Status:* emerged from nothingness at beginning of world. *Career:* existed in Ginnungagap; nourished first Frost Giant, Ymir, with her milk; licked Bor, father of the gods, out of primeval ice. *Personality:* maternal; passive. *Distinguishing Features:* a giant cow. *Supernatural Attributes:* neverending supply of nourishing milk. Page 8.

Associations (if any): Things linked with the character.

AEGIR (a-gear). *Category:* Vanir god. *Family Status:* m. Ran; nine daughters. *Career:* god of the sea; made his fortune with treasure from shipwrecks; gathers drowning victims in net and entertains them in his underwater hall; brewer to the gods. *Personality:* unpredictable; calm at times; stormy moods. *Distinguishing Features:* lives underwater. *Supernatural Attributes:* controls the waves through his nine daughters; directs the winds. Page 82, 95, 102.

AESIR (a-seer). *Category:* gods. *Family Status:* s. and d. of Odin. *Career:* warriors; Keepers of the Dead; judges of human behaviour; main leaders – Odin, Thor, Balder, Tyr, Frigg, Sif. *Personality:* varied. *Supernatural Attributes:* super-human strength and courage; shape-changing ability; possess many magic weapons and animals. Page 70, 73, 86.

AFI (ah-fee) "Grandfather". *Category:* human. *Family Status:* m. Amma; one s. Karl, given by Heimdall. *Career:* farmer; small landowner; chosen by gods to be ancestor of all farm-owners. *Personality:* hardworking; generous; worthy. Page 83.

AGNAR (ag-nar).i. *Category:* human. *Family Status:* s. of King of the Goths. *Career:* heir to throne of the Goths; ship-wrecked with brother, Geirrod, when ten years old; cared for by Odin and Frigg in disguise; favourite of Frigg; set adrift and abandoned by Geirrod at end of their journey home; survived but led wild life; became smith to King Hjalprek of Jutland. *Personality:* adventurous; fond of bad company, wild women, drinking etc. Page 100.

AGNAR (ag-nar).ii. *Category:* human. *Family Status:* s. of Geirrod. *Career:* pitied Odin when he was tied to a spit in Geirrod's court and gave him a drink; inherited throne of the Goths. *Personality:* kind-hearted. *Supernatural Attributes:* enjoyed protection of Odin for his act of kindness. Page 100.

AI (ah-ee) "Great Grandfather". *Category:* human. *Family Status:* m. Edda; one s. Thrall, granted them by Heimdall. *Career:* poor labourer; given by gods to be ancestor to all labourers. *Personality:* humble; generous. Page 83.

ALTI (al-tee). *Category:* human. *Family Status:* m. Gudrun; several sons. *Career:* Gudrun's second husband; avenged death of her first husband, Sigurd, by killing his murderer; became greedy for gold Gudrun's family had and murdered Gudrun's brothers for it; was despatched by Gudrun in revenge. *Personality:* weak; easily dominated; avaricious. *Associations:* linked to the real character, Attila the Hun. Page 99.

AMMA (am-ah) "Grandmother". *Category:* human. *Family Status:* m. Afi; one s. Karl, granted to them by Heimdall. *Career:* farmer's wife; chosen by gods to raise ancestor of all farm-owners. *Personality:* maternal; generous. Page 83.

ANDVARI (and-varri). *Category:* Dwarf. *Career:* gold-collector; keeper of magic ring; forced to give all his treasure to Loki to pay ransom for death of Hreidmar's son; cursed gold and ring when taken from him. *Personality:* greedy; solitary; vindictive. *Distinguishing Features:* took form of a pike and lived in dark pool in Svartalfheim. *Supernatural Attributes:* shape-changing ability; cursing and spell-casting. Page 98.

ANGANTYR (an-gan-tier). *Category:* human. *Career:* pretender to Ottar's throne; entered contest with Ottar that each should recite correctly a list of his ancestors; lost contest and throne. *Personality:* ambitious. Page 96.

ANGRBODA (anger-bodda) "Distress-Bringer". *Category:* Giantess. *Family Status:* lo. of Loki; three children, Fenrir, Hel, Jormungand. *Career:* enemy of the gods; had much disapproved-of affair with Loki; produced monstrous children she could not control. *Personality:* evil. *Distinguishing Features:* giant size. *Supernatural Attributes:* giving birth to monsters. Page 81, 88.

ASK (assk) "Ash". *Category:* human. *Family Status:* m. Embla; many children. *Career:* created from ash branch found on beach by Odin; given life; first human. *Personality:* simple; obedient. *Distinguishing Features:* mortal. Page 75.

AUDUMLA (ow-doom-la) "Nourisher". *Category:* supernatural animal. *Family

Status: emerged from nothingness at beginning of world. **Career:** existed in Ginnungagap; nourished first Frost Giant, Ymir, with her milk; licked Bor, father of the gods, out of primeval ice. **Personality:** maternal; passive. **Distinguishing Features:** a giant cow. **Supernatural Attributes:** neverending supply of nourishing milk. **Page 74.**

BALDER (bal-der). **Category:** Aesir god. **Family Status:** s. of Odin and Frigg; m. Nanna; one s. Forseti. **Career:** giving advice; reconciling enemies; called Bright One; hated by Loki for his popularity; developed morbid fancies about death; Frigg made everything in the world swear not to harm him (except mistletoe, which she missed); dreams of death realized when Loki gave mistletoe dart to Hod to throw at him; his death heralded Ragnarok, the Doom of the gods. **Personality:** wise; gentle; beloved. **Distinguishing Features:** fair hair; shining face. **Supernatural Attributes:** immunity to all harmful things, except mistletoe. **Page 80, 89, 101, 103.**

BERGELMIR (bare-ghel-mere). **Category:** Giant. **Family Status:** father to all Giants. **Career:** escaped drowning in Ymir's blood when Ymir killed by Odin; rode away in hollow tree-trunk with wife; replenished Giant population. **Personality:** strong survival instinct. **Distinguishing Features:** enormous proportions. **Page 75.**

BESTLA (best-lah). **Category:** Giantess. **Family Status:** d. of Ymir; m. Bor; three s. Odin, Vili, Ve. **Career:** Frost Giantess; mother to the first gods. **Page 74.**

BOLVERK (boll-verk). **Category:** god/Giant. **Family Status:** Odin in disguise. **Career:** Odin became Bolverk to obtain Mead of Poetry; tricked the Giant Braugi's servants into killing each other; helped Braugi in the fields then forced him to tell where his brother kept the Mead of Poetry in payment; wooed Giantess Gunnlod who was guarding the Mead; persuaded her to give him a sip, then sucked it all into his mouth and flew off in form of an eagle. **Personality:** charming; persuasive; fatally attractive to Giantesses. **Distinguishing Features:** giant size; v. handsome. **Supernatural Attributes:** shape-changing ability. **Page 97.**

BOR (bore). **Category:** supernatural being. **Family Status:** s. of Buri, who was licked from the original ice by Audumla, the giant cow; m. Bor; three s. Odin, Vili, Ve. **Career:** father of the gods. **Page 74.**

BRAGI (bra-ghee). **Category:** god. **Family Status:** s. of Odin and Frigg; m. Idunn. **Career:** god of poetry, eloquence and wisdom; greets new arrivals in Valhalla and sings songs celebrating their deeds. **Personality:** intellectual; poetic. **Supernatural Attributes:** inspiring humans to poetry. **Page 77.**

BRAUGI (brow-ghee). **Category:** Giant. **Family Status:** brother to Gilling and Suttung. **Career:** used by Odin to get at the Mead of Poetry; Odin, in disguise as Giant, Bolverk, killed all his servants,

then offered to work for him in return for sip of Mead owned by Suttung; agreed to bargain, but could not keep it as Suttung would not give Bolverk any Mead; forced to reveal where Mead was hidden and Odin stole it. **Personality:** gullible. **Distinguishing Features:** v. big. **Page 97.**

BROKK (brock). **Category:** Dwarf. **Career:** superb smith and jeweller; maker (with Eitri) of golden boar Gullinbursti, Odin's gold arm-ring and Thor's hammer Mjollnir; made wager of Loki's head that his work was as good as any other Dwarf's; gods agreed but Brokk was denied his prize when Loki said he could take the head but must not cut off any of his neck; this was impossible; sewed up Loki's mouth in revenge. **Personality:** aggressive; proud of his skill; somewhat bragging. **Distinguishing Features:** small; unattractive and blackened from the smithy. **Page 90.**

BRYNHILD (brin-hild). **Category:** supernatural being/human. **Family Status:** servant to Odin; lo. of Sigurd; m. Gunnar. **Career:** Valkyrie; liked to visit Earth in swan disguise to swim; had swan feathers stolen by a man who made her change the course of a battle before he would return them; this caused a favourite of Odin's to lose battle; stripped of Valkyrie status; placed in magic sleep in castle surrounded by fire; rescued by and was to marry Sigurd; became victim of curse of Andvari's gold, which Sigurd owned; cheated of happiness by evil plans of Queen Grimhild, who wanted the gold; Sigurd married Grimhild's d. Gudrun instead of her; Brynhild forced to marry Gunnar; in desperation, arranged Sigurd's death; committed suicide. **Personality:** unlucky; tragic figure; latterly, bitter and vengeful. **Distinguishing Features:** great warrior as a Valkyrie; v. beautiful. **Associations:** she was called Brunnhilde in Richard Wagner's opera version of the story of Sigurd and the ring, called "Der Ring des Nibelungen". **Page 99.**

BURI (boo-ree). **Category:** supernatural being. **Family Status:** licked from the primeval ice by the giant cow, Audumla; produced one s. Bor. **Career:** grandfather to the first gods. **Page 74.**

DARK ELVES. See **ELVES.**

DAY. **Category:** Giant. **Family Status:** s. of Night. **Career:** followed his mother in horse-drawn chariot, encircling the world once every 24 hours. **Personality:** reliable. **Distinguishing Features:** brought light. **Page 75.**

DWARFS. **Category:** supernatural beings. **Family Status:** created by gods from maggots crawling in the flesh of Ymir. **Career:** usually skilled craftsmen; hoarding gold and precious jewels; trying to win favour

of the gods; attempting to woo goddesses; usually enemies of Giants. **Personality:** greedy; cunning; sometimes downright evil. **Distinguishing Features:** small stature; ugly features; sometimes physical deformity. **Page 71, 75, 90, 98.**

EAST. **Category:** Dwarf. **Career:** holding up one corner of the sky with North, South and West. **Page 75.**

EDDA (edda) "Great Grandmother". **Category:** human. **Family Status:** m. Ai; one s. Thrall, granted them by Heimdall. **Career:** poor labourer's wife; chosen to bring up the ancestor of all farm labourers. **Personality:** humble. **Page 83.**

EITRI (a-tree). **Category:** Dwarf. **Career:** metal-worker/smith; helped Brokk make the hammer Mjollnir, gold boar Gullinbursti and gold arm-ring. **Page 90.**

ELVES. **Category:** supernatural beings. **Career:** can be Light or Dark; Light Elves live in Alfheim and are good, helpful; Dark Elves live in caves and holes of Svartalfheim and are mischievous trouble-makers. **Distinguishing Features:** small; human-shaped. **Page 66, 71, 73.**

EMBLA (em-bla) "Elm". **Category:** human. **Family Status:** m. Ask; many children. **Career:** first human woman; created by Odin from elm branch found on beach; given life; populated Earth with humans. **Personality:** simple, obedient. **Distinguishing Features:** mortal. **Page 75.**

ENNA (en-ah). **Category:** human. **Family Status:** m. Jarl; many children. **Career:** chieftain's daughter; married and became ancestor to the noble classes. **Personality:** dignified. **Page 83.**

FAFNIR (fahf-near). **Category:** human. **Family Status:** s. of Hreidmar. **Career:** farmer; visited by Odin, Loki and Honir in disguise; gods accidentally killed his brother (disguised as an otter); Fafnir, his father and brother Regin bound the gods while they slept and demanded compensation; Loki got them gold from Andvari the Dwarf; Andvari cursed the gold, esp. a gold ring; driven by the curse, Fafnir killed his father to get the gold; refused to share it with Regin; ran away and turned himself into a dragon to guard treasure; killed by his nephew, Sigurd, on instigation of Regin. **Personality:** unremarkable until affected by curse; then greedy; ruthless; selfish. **Distinguishing Features:** became a dragon. **Supernatural Attributes:** wizardry, learnt from his father; shape-changing. **Page 98.**

FARBAUTI (far-bowt-ee) "Cruel Striker". **Category:** Giant. **Family Status:** one s. Loki. **Distinguishing Features:** immense size. **Page 81.**

FATHIR (fath-ear) "Father". **Category:** human. **Family Status:** m. Mothir; one s. Jarl, given to them by Heimdall. **Career:** rich landowner; chosen by gods to raise the ancestor of all nobles. **Personality:** generous; noble. **Page 83.**

FENRIR (fen-rear). *Category:* monster. *Family Status:* s. of Loki and Giantess Angrboda. *Career:* enemy of the gods; allowed to roam free by the gods, even after his brother and sister (Jormungand and Hel) were banished; grew huge and violent until he was a threat to the gods; gods tricked him into testing his strength on a magic rope made by Dwarfs; bound by the rope and could not break free; bit off Tyr's hand, which had been placed in his mouth as assurance against trickery; was kept prisoner underground; future role to break free at Ragnarok and kill Odin; destined to be killed by Odin's son, Vidar. *Personality:* vicious; malicious trouble-maker. *Distinguishing Features:* a huge, fierce wolf. *Supernatural Attributes:* incredible strength. **Page 81, 88.**

FJALAR (fyah-lar). *Category:* Dwarf. *Family Status:* brother of Galar. *Career:* craftsman; perpetrator of evil deeds with his brother; murdered Kvasir and made Mead of Poetry from his blood; drowned the Giant Gilling and killed his wife; saved his own skin by giving the Mead to Gilling's brother, Suttung, when he came for revenge. *Personality:* heartless; treacherous; self-seeking. *Distinguishing Features:* small; ugly. **Page 97.**

FORSETI (force-ett-ee). *Category:* god. *Family Status:* s. of Balder and Nanna. *Career:* god of justice; arbitrator in quarrels. *Personality:* high moral standards; good judgement; fair. **Page 80.**

FREYJA (fray-ah). *Category:* Vanir goddess. *Family Status:* d. of Njord; sister of Freyr; m. Od. *Career:* fertility goddess; goddess of love and beauty; abandoned by Od and mourned him permanently; moved to Asgard as part of pact to end war between gods; taught magic to the Aesir; very fond of gold and jewels; took many lovers; bothered by unwanted attentions of Giants and Dwarfs; became goddess of the Dead as punishment for lowering herself to spending the night with four Dwarfs to obtain the necklace, Brisingamen, that they had made; surveyed battlefields and chose warriors to be entertained in her hall, Sessrumnir; often teased by Loki; fell in love with a human, Ottar; lived with him on Earth and helped him secure his throne by magic; often called Syr, meaning sow, her emblem. *Personality:* proud; judgement affected by desire for beautiful objects. *Distinguishing Features:* cries golden tears. *Supernatural Attributes:* magic powers; can fly when her spirit puts on falcon skin she possesses; drives chariot drawn by two cats, which fly through the air. **Page 84, 86, 89, 91, 96.**

FREYR (fray-er). *Category:* Vanir god. *Family Status:* s. of Njord; brother to Freyja. m. Gerd. *Career:* god of fertility and plenty; protected warriors in battle; moved to Asgard with Njord and Freyja in pact to end war between the gods; paid for his disobedience in sitting on Odin's throne to survey the Nine Worlds, which was forbidden, when he saw and fell in love with Giantess, Gerd; suffered horribly for love until Njord helped him woo Gerd and eventually marry her; will die at Ragnarok because he gives away his magic sword to Skirnir. *Personality:* bold; inquisitive; non-violent. *Supernatural Attributes:* owns golden boar, Gullinbursti; has magic ship, Skidbladnir; uses sword that can move through the air of its own accord. **Page 85, 90.**

FRIGG (frig). *Category:* Aesir goddess. *Family Status:* m. Odin; two s. Balder, Bragi. *Career:* Queen of the gods; Mother goddess; mourns death of Balder; helps women in labour; likes to visit Earth in disguise and intervene in human lives; holds her own with Odin – taught him a lesson when they argued over which of their two foster-sons, Agnar and Geirrod, had turned out worse. *Personality:* regal; independent; clever. *Supernatural Attributes:* shape-changing. *Associations:* the English word Friday comes from "Frigg's day". **Page 77, 78, 101.**

FULLA (full-ah). *Category:* goddess. *Career:* maidservant to Frigg; sent to warn King Geirrod of the approach of a magician, who is really Odin in disguise. *Personality:* willing; obedient. **Page 100.**

GALAR (gay-lar). See **FJALAR**.

GARM (garm). *Category:* monster. *Career:* guardian of the gates of Hel; seeing off unwanted visitors; will lead the dead out of Hel to fight the gods at Ragnarok; he will rip Tyr's throat out and be killed by the god at the same time. *Personality:* ferocious; unthinkingly violent; evil. *Distinguishing Features:* a huge hound with a blood-stained breast. **Page 73, 103.**

GEFION (ghev-yon). *Category:* goddess. *Family Status:* lo. of a Giant; four s. giant oxen. *Career:* goddess of ploughing; famous for teaching King Gylfi a lesson; was in disguise as an old woman and shared her food and fire with him; he offered her as much of the kingdom of Sweden as she could plough with four oxen in one day in thanks; she got her sons to plough a huge area and towed it away to Denmark, where it formed the island of Zealand. *Personality:* moral; sensitive to feelings of others. **Page 96-97.**

GEIRROD (gay-rod).i. *Category:* human. *Family Status:* s. of King of the Goths; one s. Agnar. *Career:* shipwrecked with his brother, Agnar, when eight years old; cared for by Odin and Frigg in disguise; became Odin's favourite; jumped overboard, taking oars and abandoning Agnar to drift in the boat in which they returned home; went home, claimed Agnar was dead and was made heir to the throne; became king but ruled badly; Odin came to court in disguise to test his behaviour and was tied to a spit between two fires; Geirrod got his just desserts – Odin was furious and caused him to trip on his own sword and kill himself. *Personality:* wicked; unjust; sly; ungrateful. **Page 100.**

GEIRROD (gay-rod).ii. *Category:* Giant. *Family Status:* two d. Gjalp, Greip. *Career:* sworn enemy of the gods; captured Loki who was wearing Freyja's falcon skin; made him promise to bring Thor to him unarmed; his daughters tried to kill Thor on his way to their hall; they failed; daughters killed by Thor; attacked Thor with red-hot iron but the god threw it back and he was killed. *Personality:* evil; scheming; over-confident. *Distinguishing Features:* very large. **Page 91.**

GERD (gird). *Category:* Giantess. *Family Status:* m. Freyr. *Career:* Frost Giantess; born enemy to the gods; spotted by Freyr when he looked at Jotunheim from Odin's throne; wooed for Freyr by Skirnir; indifferent to Freyr's love; agreed to meet Freyr after Skirnir made threats on her father's life; strength of Freyr's love melted her icy heart and she married him; went to live in Asgard and was happy. *Personality:* naturally cold; frigid; became loving. *Distinguishing Features:* v. large; shining beauty. **Page 85.**

GIANTS/GIANTESSES. *Category:* supernatural beings. *Career:* may be Frost, Fire, or Mountain Giants; with a few exceptions they are enemies to the gods (esp. Thor); war-making, cheating or fooling the gods are their favourite pastimes; their stronghold, Utgard, is said to be either in the barren mountains of Jotunheim, East of Midgard, or beyond the Ocean; *Personality:* Frost Giants extremely cold characters; Fire Giants hot-tempered; Mountain Giants hard as rocks; all short-tempered; quick to physical violence. *Distinguishing Features:* enormous size; frosty, fiery or rocky appearance, depending on type. *Supernatural Attributes:* strength equalling the gods'; shape-changing ability. **Page 71, 73, 75, 87, 89, 91, 92, 93, 94, 95, 96, 97, 102.**

GILLING (ghill-ing). *Category:* Giant. *Career:* he and his wife killed by evil Dwarfs, Fjalar and Galar for no recorded reason; his brother, Suttung went to avenge his death and got Mead of Poetry as a pay-off; his other brother Braugi was used by Odin to obtain the Mead by a trick. *Personality:* gullible. *Distinguishing Features:* huge stature. **Page 97.**

GIUKI (gyook-ee). *Category:* human. *Family Status:* m. Grimhild; one s. Gunnar; one d. Gudrun. *Career:* King of the Nibelungs; party to his wife's plan to get Sigurd's treasure by making him forget Brynhild and marry his own daughter, Gudrun. *Personality:* weak. **Page 99.**

GRID (greed). *Category:* Giantess. *Career:* ally of the gods; warned naive Thor against Geirrod when he stayed at her house with Loki on his way to Geirrod's hall; gave Thor a magic belt and iron gauntlets. *Personality:* wise; kind. *Distinguishing Features:* v. big. **Page 91.**

GRIMHILD (grim-hild). *Category:* human. *Family Status:* m. Giuki; one s. Gunnar; one d. Gudrun. *Career:* Queen of the Nibelungs; caught in the curse of Andvari's gold; desired to get the gold from Sigurd; gave him a love potion so he forgot Brynhild, his betrothed, and married her daughter, Gudrun; got the gold but brought the curse down on her family and there followed many violent deaths. *Personality:* grasping; opportunist; ambitious; domineering. **Page 99.**

GRIMNIR (grim-near). *Category:* human/god. *Career:* Odin in disguise; magician; form taken by Odin when visiting King Geirrod's court to test his treatment of guests; was extremely badly treated – tied to a spit between two fires; was pitied by Geirrod's son, who gave him a drink; burst out of this disguise; despatched Geirrod by making him stumble onto his own sword. *Personality:* apparently amiable and wise. *Distinguishing Features:* wore blue cloak and large hat; dogs would not bark at him. *Supernatural Attributes:* magician; possessed all the powers of Odin. **Page 100.**

GUDRUN (good-roon). *Category:* human. *Family Status:* d. of King Giuki and Queen Grimhild; m. Sigurd; m. Alti; several sons. *Career:* entered her mother's plot to marry Sigurd for his treasure; thus became victim of curse of Andvari's gold; Sigurd killed by jealous Brynhild; married Alti and made him kill Sigurd's murderers; Alti killed Gudrun's brothers to have all the gold for himself; she arranged Alti's death in revenge; met a violent death herself, as did all her sons; these deaths ended Andvari's curse. *Personality:* strong-willed; ambitious; unscrupulous. **Page 99.**

GULLFAXI (gool-fax-ee) "Golden Mane". *Category:* supernatural animal. *Career:* steed of the Giant Hrungnir; took part in a race with Odin on Sleipnir; passed into Thor's hands when the god slew Hrungnir; was desired by Odin, but Thor gave him to his own son, Magni. *Distinguishing Features:* superb horse with golden mane. *Supernatural Attributes:* could gallop through air. **Page 92.**

GULLINBURSTI (gool-in-burst-ee) "Golden Bristles". *Category:* supernatural animal. *Career:* made by Dwarfs, Brokk and Eitri; given to Loki, who gave it to Freyr; pulled Freyr's chariot and became his symbol. *Distinguishing Features:* a boar with golden bristles. *Personality:* fierce. *Supernatural Attributes:* fantastic running speed. **Page 90.**

GULLTOP (gool-top). *Category:* supernatural animal. *Career:* Heimdall's mount. *Distinguishing Features:* magnificent horse with golden mane. *Supernatural Attributes:* great speed; flying powers. **Page 83.**

GULLVEIG (gool-vague). *Category:* Vanir goddess. *Career:* mistress of magic; seeress; catalyst in war between the gods; she visited the Aesir and boasted about her magic skills but would not tell her secrets; was murdered and thrown on the fire by the Aesir; by her magic powers she emerged unscathed; the Aesir tried to

burn her twice more but finally allowed her to go free; given a new name, Heid, meaning Gleaming One; she recounted her shameful treatment to the Vanir and ensuing argument with the Aesir caused war between the gods. *Personality:* boastful; infuriating. *Supernatural Attributes:* gift of prophecy; magic powers; healing ability. **Page 86.**

GUNNAR (goon-ar). *Category:* human. *Family Status:* s. of King Giuki and Queen Grimhild; m. Brynhild. *Career:* desired Brynhild; took advantage of his mother's plan to marry his sister to Sigurd to get Brynhild for himself; used Sigurd to woo Brynhild. *Personality:* mother-dominated; insensitive. **Page 99.**

GUNNLOD (goon-lod). *Category:* Giantess. *Family Status:* d. of Suttung. *Career:* had lonely task of guarding the Mead of Poetry in underground cavern; poor girl fooled by Odin who courted her in his disguise as a handsome Giant; was persuaded to give him a sip of Mead; he took it all and disappeared; she was heartbroken; had to face Suttung's extreme anger. *Personality:* easily taken in; not too bright. *Distinguishing Features:* enormous build. **Page 97.**

GYLFI (ghill-vee). *Category:* human. *Career:* King of Sweden; lost a large chunk of his kingdom when he got involved with goddess, Gefion; she was in disguise as a beggarwoman; he talked with her all night and was so impressed by her wisdom that he offered her as much of his kingdom as she could plough with four oxen in a day as a reward; was taught a resounding lesson when Gefion used supernatural oxen and dragged away a huge tract of land; she towed it to Denmark, where it became island of Zealand; left a hole in Sweden which became Lake Malar. *Personality:* caring; well-meaning but unwise. **Page 96-97.**

HARBARD (hah-bard). *Category:* human/god. *Career:* ferryman; disguise chosen by Odin to get his own back on Thor for not giving him the Giant Hrungnir's horse; refused to carry Thor across river, told him lies about his family and drove him to a fury. *Personality:* irritating; unpleasant. **Page 79.**

HATI (hah-tee). *Category:* supernatural animal. *Family Status:* s. of Giantess of Iron Wood. *Career:* chasing Moon across sky; destined to catch and swallow Moon at Ragnarok. *Personality:* single-minded; relentless. *Distinguishing Features:* he is a huge wolf. *Supernatural Attributes:* runs through the air. **Page 75, 103.**

HEID (hade). See **GULLVEIG.**

HEIMDALL (hame-dall). *Category:* Vanir god. *Family Status:* s. of nine maidens, possibly daughters of Aegir and Ran. *Career:* guardian of Bifrost, the Rainbow bridge between Asgard and Midgard; warned the gods of the approach of strangers; constant enemy to Loki; founder of the breeds of thrall, farmer and noble when he visited Earth in disguise as Rig and gave sons to three families typical of the three types. *Personality:* noble;

serious-minded. *Supernatural Attributes:* super-fine hearing and sight – can hear the grass grow and see for a hundred miles; needs little sleep; possesses gold-maned stallion, Gulltop, who can fly. **Page 73, 81, 82, 89, 93, 103.**

HEL (hell). *Category:* supernatural being. *Family Status:* d. of Loki and Giantess Angrboda. *Career:* enemy to the gods; banished to Land of the Dead (also called Hel) when the Norns warned the gods against her; became Queen of the Dead and ruled over those who died other than in battle; said Balder could return from the dead if everything in the Nine Worlds mourned for him – it was her father who would not cry so she could refuse to release Balder; she will lead dead souls against the gods at Ragnarok. *Personality:* cold; stern; unforgiving. *Distinguishing Features:* horrifically deformed – beautiful woman to the waist, dead and rotting below. **Page 73, 81, 88, 101, 103.**

HERMOD (hair-mod). *Category:* Aesir god. *Family Status:* s. of Odin. *Career:* unexceptional until Frigg needed a volunteer to visit Hel to try and get Balder back; he successfully bargained with Hel for release of Balder, as long as every living thing would mourn for him; foiled when Loki, disguised as Giantess, refused to weep. *Personality:* honourable; brave. **Page 101.**

HILDISVINI (hill-dee-sveen-ee). *Category:* supernatural animal. *Family Status:* belonged to Freyja. *Career:* servant and symbol to Freyja; lent his form to Ottar when he went with Freyja to visit Giantess Hyndla to obtain list of Ottar's ancestors. *Distinguishing Features:* he is a boar. *Supernatural Attributes:* can travel at great speed. **Page 96.**

HJORDIS (hyaw-deess). *Category:* human. *Family Status:* d. of Hreidmar; m. Sigmund; one s. Sigurd. *Career:* Sigurd died before birth of Sigmund; mother and son cared for by her brother, Regin. *Personality:* quiet; submissive. **Page 98.**

HOD (hod). *Category:* Aesir god. *Family Status:* s. of Odin and Frigg. *Career:* little known of his career – hampered by blindness; unfairly used by Loki to murder Balder; Loki gave him poison mistletoe dart to join in game of throwing things at Balder to see how they bounced safely off him; Loki guided Hod's aim and dart killed Balder; although innocent of evil intent, Hod was killed by Odin's son, Vali, in revenge; justice will be done when Hod returns from dead after Ragnarok to be among new gods. *Personality:* solitary; outsider; *Distinguishing Features:* blindness. **Page 101, 103.**

HONIR (ho-near). *Category:* Aesir god. *Career:* great warrior; went to live in Vanaheim when gods swapped leaders after their war; Vanir not particularly impressed by him – he was strong but not clever; Mimir (his companion) suffered for his shortcomings; Vanir cut off Mimir's head and sent it back to Odin to show their disappointment. *Personality:* aggressive; none too bright. *Distinguishing Features:* warrior dress. **Page 86.**

HREIDMAR (hrade-mar). *Category:* human. *Family Status:* three s. Regin, Fafnir, Otter. *Career:* farmer; magician; Otter, disguised as an otter, was unwittingly killed by Loki, who was visiting Earth with Odin and Honir; Hreidmar demanded large sum of gold in compensation; Loki fetched him the treasure of Andvari the Dwarf; Andvari cursed the gold, esp. a gold ring; the curse took effect when Fafnir killed Hreidmar in his greed for the gold; this was the start of long chain of death and violence associated with Andvari's gold. *Personality:* shrewd; avaricious. **Page 98.**

HRUNGNIR (hroong-near). *Category:* Giant. *Career:* challenged Odin to a race; their horses evenly matched; ended up in Asgard having a friendly drink together; he got drunk and rowdy and thrown out by Thor; arranged single combat with Thor; threw whetstone at Thor but killed by Mjollnir; body fell on top of Thor and had to be removed by Thor's son Magni; pieces of shattered whetstone lodged in Thor's head, causing headaches. *Personality:* competitive; given to over-indulgence in alcohol. *Distinguishing Features:* great size. **Page 92.**

HUGINN (hoog-in) "Thought" and **MUNINN** (moon-in) "Memory". *Category:* supernatural animals. *Career:* news reporters to Odin; they fly through the Nine Worlds collecting information, then whisper it in Odin's ears; when not investigating, are to be found on Odin's shoulders. *Personality:* nosy; tireless. *Distinguishing Features:* they are giant ravens. **Page 76.**

HYMIR (him-ear). *Category:* Giant. *Family Status:* m. Tyr's mother. *Career:* best-known for obstructing Thor and Tyr when they came to fetch a cauldron for Aegir to make ale in for the gods; he and Thor went fishing after Thor polished off all the meat there was in the house; got a fright when Thor attracted Jormungand to his hook and there was a mighty struggle; reluctant to let Thor have the cauldron he requested; said the god could have it if he could break a magic glass Hymir possessed; Thor broke magic spell, and glass, by throwing it at Hymir's head; Hymir gave him the cauldron with bad grace; sent many-headed giants after the gods to attack them, but Thor dealt with them. *Personality:* grumpy; ill-will towards gods; grudging. *Distinguishing Features:* enormous build. **Page 95.**

HYNDLA (hinnd-la). *Category:* Giantess. *Career:* antipathy towards gods; keeper of complete list of Ottar's ancestors; famed for her unhelpfulness when Freyja came to her wanting list; was persuaded to hand list over, but would not give Ottar a sip of magic Memory Beer so he could remember the names; went too far in antagonizing the goddess; Freyja lost her temper and threw ring of fire round Hyndla, which closed in on her; Giantess

gave in and handed over Beer; placed curse on Ottar, but ineffective as he had Freyja's protection. *Personality:* bad-tempered; obstructive; strong instinct for self-preservation. *Distinguishing Features:* gigantic proportions. *Supernatural Attributes:* possession of magic Memory Beer. **Page 96.**

HYRROKIN (hirro-kin). *Category:* Giantess. *Career:* friend to the gods; renowned for pushing Balder and Nanna's funeral boat out to sea; nobody else could move it as it was so laden with treasure. *Personality:* sympathetic; helpful. *Distinguishing Features:* hugeness. **Page 101.**

IDUNN (id-doon). *Category:* Aesir goddess. *Family Status:* m. to Bragi. *Career:* keeper of golden apples that keep the gods young; led by Loki into near-disaster when he tricked her into leaving Asgard with her apples;

this was part of a deal he had made with the Giant Thiazi to escape from his clutches; she was captured and imprisoned by Thiazi; gods started to grow old and weak without her apples to eat; was rescued by Loki, flying in Freyja's falcon skin; he turned her into a nut to carry her in his beak; brought her back safely to Asgard; Thiazi followed and was killed by gods. *Personality:* good; responsible; naive. *Distinguishing Features:* young and beautiful. *Supernatural Attributes:* responsibility for golden apples of youth. **Page 77, 89.**

JARL (yarl). *Category:* human. *Family Status:* s. of Fathir and Mothir, given them by Heimdall; m. Enna; many children. *Career:* brought up as son of wealthy parents; grew handsome and strong; when out hunting one day, was met by Heimdall, who told him some of the secrets of the gods so he became esp. wise; Heimdall said he had a right to win lands and rule men and this is what he did; his descendants were the class of nobles. *Personality:* valiant; noble. **Page 83.**

JARNSAXA (yarn-sax-a). *Category:* Giantess. *Family Status:* lo. of Thor; two s. Magni and Modi. *Career:* friendly to gods; Thor's mistress; cared for their sons. *Personality:* kind; maternal. *Distinguishing Features:* large size. **Page 93.**

JORMUNGAND (yore-mun-gand). *Category:* monster. *Family Status:* s. of Loki and Giantess, Angrboda. *Career:* trouble-making enemy of the gods; thrown into Ocean by Odin, after warning from Norns that he was a danger;  grew bigger and bigger until he circled the Earth and could take his own tail in his mouth; posed great threat to sailors who ventured into deep waters; was once

hooked by Thor when he was fishing with Hymir; there was a great struggle, but Thor bashed him on the head and he retreated; still holds grudge against Thor and they are destined to meet again at Ragnarok; it is predicted that Thor will kill him, only to die himself from Jormungand's poison. *Personality:* malevolent; menacing; danger to humans and gods. *Distinguishing Features:* gigantic serpent — called the World Serpent. *Supernatural Attributes:* fatal venom. **Page 73, 81, 88, 95, 103.**

JORTH (yorth) "Earth". *Category:* goddess. *Family Status:* lo. of Odin; one s. Thor. *Career:* Mother goddess; could simply be Frigg by another name. **Page 78.**

KARL (karl). *Category:* human. *Family Status:* s. of Afi and Amma, given to them by Heimdall; many sons. *Career:* raised as farm-owner; destined to be ancestor of all farm-owners. *Personality:* down to earth; hard-working; practical. **Page 83.**

KOBOLDS (co-bolds). *Category:* supernatural beings. *Career:* live near humans in barns and stables; sometimes helpful, sometimes a pest depending on how they are treated. *Personality:* elusive; mischievous. *Distinguishing Features:* small; human-shaped. **Page 71.**

KVASIR (kvah-seer). *Category:* human. *Career:* fashioned from spittle of the gods when they all spat into jar to seal the peace after war between Aesir and Vanir; inherited wisdom of the gods and was consulted for his good advice throughout the world; treacherously murdered by Dwarfs Fjalar and Galar; they brewed the Mead of Poetry from his blood; the Mead inspired wisdom and poetry in those who drank it; it passed into the hands of the Giant, Suttung, and eventually Odin obtained it for the gods by trickery. *Personality:* wise; trusting. *Supernatural Attributes:* wisdom of the gods. **Page 97.**

LAUFEY (lowf-ee). *Category:* Giantess. *Family Status:* m. Farbauti; s. incl. Loki. *Career:* mother of Loki. **Page 81.**

LIF (leaf) and **LIFTHRASIR** (leaf-thrass-ear). *Category:* humans. *Family Status:* m. to each other. *Career:* escaped into branches of Yggdrasil at Ragnarok and survived to re-populate Earth. *Personality:* strong survival instinct; opportunists. **Page 103.**

LIGHT ELVES. See **ELVES.**

LOGI (lo-ghee). *Category:* Giant. *Career:* enemy to the gods; well-known for incident when Thor and Loki visited Utgard when his form was borrowed by Fire to beat Loki in eating contest; Fire consumes everything, so won the contest for Giants. *Personality:* competitive. *Distinguishing Features:* great size. **Page 94.**

LOKI (lo-kee). *Category:* Giant/god. *Family Status:* s. of Giants Farbauti and Laufey; lo. of Angrboda and had three children, Jormungand, Fenrir, Hel; m. Sigyn and had two sons, Vali and Narvi. *Career:* blood-brother to Odin; lived in Asgard and had god-like status; loved adventures, mischief, trickery and disguise; amused the gods (except Heimdall); went with them on adventures – to Utgard with Thor; to Earth with Odin and Honir; provoked Andvari's curse by stealing his gold; always in trouble with Giants; compromised others to save himself – caused kidnapping of Idunn and got Thor into danger with the Giant Geirrod; produced magic, eight-legged horse, Sleipnir, while in disguise as a mare; got treasures from the Dwarfs; gradually embittered as gods tired of his behaviour and began to laugh at him; jealous of Balder and caused his death; prevented Balder's return from dead by refusing to weep for him; avoided gods after this but later turned up at a feast and made spiteful speech against them; ran off but was caught; tied to rocks; a serpent that dropped venom on his face placed overhead; Sigyn tried to catch poison but when it hit him he writhed and the Earth shook; he was fated to break free and fight the gods at Ragnarok. *Personality:* mischievous, becoming evil; daring; annoying; strong instinct for self-preservation. *Distinguishing Features:* small; handsome; agile; often called Shape-Changer. *Supernatural Attributes:* great gift for shape-changing. **Page 81, 83, 87, 88, 89, 90, 91, 93, 94, 98, 101, 102, 103.**

MAGNI (mag-nee). *Category:* god. *Family Status:* s. of Thor and Giantess Jarnsaxa. *Career:* extremely strong from birth; at only three years old he rescued Thor who was trapped under body of the Giant Hrungnir; Thor gave him Hrungnir's horse, Gold Mane, in thanks; he will survive Ragnarok and inherit Thor's hammer; will be one of the new gods. *Personality:* brave and bold. **Page 92, 103.**

MIMIR (mee-meer). *Category:* Aesir god. *Career:* guardian of Well of Mimir in Jotunheim, fountain of all wisdom; was v. wise; gave Odin a sip from the well, at the cost of one of his eyes; was sent with Honir to live with Vanir when gods exchanged leaders after the war between them; became victim of Vanir's disappointment in Honir, who was useless if separated from Mimir; showed their disapproval by cutting off Mimir's head and sending it back to Odin; Odin preserved it and gave it the power of speech; placed head back by Mimir's Well so it could still be consulted. *Personality:* v. knowledgeable; good teacher. *Distinguishing Features:* existed as a head only after being beheaded by Vanir. *Supernatural Attributes:* wisdom and talking ability even after head cut off. **Page 73, 86, 87.**

MODI (mode-ee). *Category:* god. *Family Status:* s. of Thor and Giantess Jarnsaxa. *Career:* no known deeds of note; his time is in the future after Ragnarok, when he will be one of the new leaders; he and his brother, Magni, will recover Thor's hammer and help world to recover. *Personality:* brave; good. **Page 103.**

MOON. *Category:* human. *Family Status:* s. of Mundulfari. *Career:* named after the planet by his father because he was v. beautiful; gods thought this was a cheek and took him away as punishment; made to drive chariot pulling the moon; pursued by terrible wolf Hati who wants to catch and destroy him. **Page 75.**

MOTHIR (moe-theer) "Mother". *Family Status:* m. Fathir; one s. Jarl, given to them as a gift from Heimdall. *Career:* nobleman's wife; chosen by Heimdall to care for Jarl, who was to be ancestor of all nobles. *Personality:* motherly. **Page 83.**

MUNDULFARI (moon-dool-farri). See **MOON.**

MUNINN (mun-in). See **HUGINN.**

NANNA (nan-ah). *Category:* Aesir goddess. *Family Status:* m. Balder; one s. Forseti. *Career:* loving wife; died of broken heart when Balder killed and cremated with him on funeral ship; arrived in Niflheim with Balder. *Personality:* gentle; loving. **Page 80, 101.**

NARVI (nar-vee). *Category:* god. *Family Status:* s. of Loki and Sigyn. *Career:* cut short by the gods when they killed him to punish Loki; was torn apart by his brother, Vali , whom gods turned into a wolf; his entrails used to bind Loki. *Personality:* unfortunate. **Page 81, 102.**

NIDHOGG (nid-hog). *Category:* monster. *Career:* enemy to the gods; attempted to destroy world by gnawing roots of Yggdrasil to kill it; guardian of Spring of Hvergelmir in Niflheim; his role after Ragnarok is to attack the corpses of wrong-doers in Nastrond. *Personality:* deliberately evil; bloodthirsty. *Distinguishing Features:* he is a dreadful dragon. **Page 73.**

NIGHT. *Category:* Giantess. *Family Status:* one s. Day. *Career:* drove horse-drawn chariot round the world once every 24 hours, bringing night. *Personality:* consistent; dutiful. *Distinguishing Features:* brought darkness. **Page 75.**

NJORD (nyord). *Category:* Vanir god. *Family Status:* one s. Freyr; one d. Freyja; m. Giantess Skadi. *Career:* god of the sea; went to live with Aesir in the exchange of leaders after war between the gods; chosen by Giantess Skadi when she was allowed to pick a husband from looking at the gods' feet; unsuccessful marriage because Skadi could not stand the sea and he could not stand her native mountains so they lived apart; helped Freyr woo his wife, Gerd. *Personality:* noble; wise; stubborn. **Page 82, 84, 85, 89.**

NORNS (nornz). *Category:* goddesses (three). *Career:* spinning destinies of humans and gods; they know everyone's Fate; sometimes known as Past, Present and Future; tend the Well of Urd in Asgard and water Yggdrasil; warned gods against Loki's brood. *Personality:* all-knowing; incorruptible. *Distinguishing Features:* v. old and wise. *Supernatural Attributes:* ability to see the future; power over lives of humans and gods. **Page 73, 88.**

NORTH. *Category:* Dwarf. *Career:* holding up the sky with Dwarfs South, East and West. **Page 75.**

OD (odd). *Category:* god. *Family Status:* m. Freyja. *Career:* obscure; he has abandoned Freyja, who mourns for him. *Personality:* apparently unfaithful and unreliable. **Page 84.**

ODIN (oh-din). *Category:* Aesir god. *Family Status:* m. Frigg; two s, Balder, Hod; many lo. incl. Rind – one s. Vali; Grid – one s. Vidar; all gods are his offspring. *Career:* King of the gods; father of all other gods and creator of humans; called Allfather; god of war; v. wise – gave up one eye to drink from Well of Mimir; sacrificed himself, died and was reborn to gain secrets of the dead; obtained the Runes and taught them to mankind; keeps watch on everything that happens in the Nine Worlds; enjoys visiting Earth in disguise; his servants, the Valkyries, choose brave warriors for him to entertain in his hall, Vallhalla. *Personality:* arrogant; stern; can be jealous and unpleasant. *Distinguishing Features:* often to be seen with the two ravens, Huginn and Muninn on his shoulders. *Supernatural Attributes:* all-seeing and all-knowing; shape-changing. **Page 76, 77, 78, 79, 80, 84, 85, 86, 88, 92, 97, 98, 100, 101, 103.**

OTTAR (ot-ar). *Category:* human. *Family Status:* lo. of Freyja. *Career:* prince; devoted to Freyja; came to Freyja's notice, she fell in love and came to Midgard to be with him; entered contest with Angantyr to decide quarrel over his throne; had to list all his ancestors correctly; Freyja turned him into her boar, Hildisvini, to visit Giantess Hyndla who had the list; with difficulty, Freyja obtained list and Memory Beer to help him remember it; Ottar cursed by Hyndla, but protected by Freyja and won the throne. *Personality:* single-minded; non-violent. *Supernatural Attributes:* Freyja's special protection. **Page 96.**

RAGING WARRIOR see VALKYRIES

RAN (ran). *Category:* Vanir goddess. *Family Status:* m. Aegir; nine daughters. *Career:* sea goddess; netted drowning victims and dragged them to sea-bed; entertained them in her hall; held feast at  which Loki insulted gods. *Personality:* variable, like the sea; unpredictable; stormy temper. **Page 82, 98, 102.**

RATATOSK (rat-ah-tosk). *Category:* supernatural animal. *Career:* running up and down trunk of Yggdrasil, trading insults between Nidhogg and eagle that sits in top branches. *Personality:* spiteful gossip; trouble-maker. *Distinguishing Features:* he is a squirrel. **Page 73.**

REGIN (ray-ghin). *Category:* human. *Family Status:* s. of Hreidmar. *Career:* farmer; helped tie up Odin, Loki and Honir after they killed one of his brothers; was refused his share of Andvari's gold after his brother, Fafnir, killed their father to get it; got revenge by bringing up his nephew, Sigurd, to kill Fafnir, which he did; then became affected by the curse on the gold, turned against Sigurd and planned to kill him; was killed by Sigurd in self-defence. *Personality:* good and kind until tainted by curse; then greedy and ruthless. **Page 98.**

RIG (rig). *Category:* human/god. *Family Status:* gave s. to Edda (Thrall); Amma (Karl); Mothir (Jarl). *Career:* human form taken by Heimdall when he visited Earth to found races of nobles, farm-owners and thralls. *Personality:* friendly; welcome guest; good judge of character. **Page 83.**

ROSKVA (rosk-va). See **THIALFI.**

SHAKER and **SHRIEKING.** See **VALKYRIES.**

SIF (siff). *Category:* Aesir goddess. *Family Status:* m. Thor. *Career:* goddess of harvest, fruitfulness and plenty; had her hair cut off by Loki; he replaced it with magic spun-gold which grew like hair, made by the Dwarfs. *Personality:* generous; somewhat vain. *Distinguishing Features:* long, gold hair. **Page 79, 90.**

SIGMUND (sig-mund). *Category:* human. *Family Status:* m. Hjordis; one s. Sigurd. *Career:* died before Sigurd born. **Page 98.**

SIGURD (sig-urd). *Category:* human. *Family Status:* grands. of Hreidmar; s. of Hjordis and Sigmund; lo. of Brynhild; m. Gudrun. *Career:* brave and adventurous but became entangled in curse of Andvari's gold; reared by his uncle, Regin, to kill his other uncle, Fafnir, for murdering Hreidmar to get the gold; Fafnir had turned into a dragon, but Sigurd killed him and ate his heart; rescued Valkyrie Brynhild from her enchanted sleep; was to marry her, but given a love potion by Grimhild of the Nibelungs, which made him forget Brynhild and marry Grimhild's daughter, Gudrun; thus the gold came into the hands of the Nibelungs; was murdered on jealous Brynhild's orders. *Personality:* courageous; good. *Supernatural Attributes:* could understand the speech of birds. **Page 98.**

SIGYN (sig-in). *Category:* goddess. *Family Status:* m. Loki; two s. Vali, Narvi. *Career:* faithful and loving wife to Loki, despite his bad behaviour; remained loyal even during his punishment – held bowl to try to keep poison off Loki's face. *Personality:* warm and loving; unquestioningly loyal. **Page 81, 102.**

SKADI (skah-dee). *Category:* Giantess. *Family Status:* d. of Thiazi; m. Njord. *Career:* great huntress; came to demand compensation when they killed her father; was offered one of the gods in marriage, to be chosen from their feet; chose Njord's feet; unhappy marriage as she hated the sea and he hated mountains so they were not happy anywhere together; eventually they separated; was given gift of laughter by Odin; placed snake above Loki to drip poison on him as part of his punishment. *Personality:* brave; independent. *Associations:* the word "Scandinavia" comes from the name Skadi. **Page 82, 89, 102.**

SKIRNIR (skeer-near). *Category:* god. *Career:* servant to Freyr; had the arm-ring Gleipnir made by the Dwarfs; made dangerous mission to Jotunheim to woo Gerd for Freyr; was given Freyr's magic sword in return; this was destined to be Freyr's downfall as he will not have sword at Ragnarok. *Personality:* daring; loyal. *Supernatural Attributes:* owner of Freyr's sword which moves through the air of its own accord. **Page 85, 89.**

SKOLL (skol). *Category:* supernatural animal. *Family Status:* s. of Witch of Iron Wood. *Career:* chasing Sun across sky in an attempt to swallow her; at Ragnarok he will succeed. *Personality:* evil single-mindedness; ferocious. *Distinguishing Features:* he is a monstrous wolf. **Page 75.**

SKRYMIR (skree-meer). *Category:* Giant. *Career:* disguise adopted by Utgard-Loki, King of the Giants, to annoy Thor's party on their way to Utgard; deliberately disturbed their sleep by snoring; sealed their food bag by magic so they could not eat; murder attempts by Thor failed because he protected himself by magic. *Personality:* unpleasant; exasperating. *Distinguishing Features:* hugeness. *Supernatural Attributes:* shape-changing; magic powers. **Page 94.**

SLEIPNIR (slape-near). *Category:* supernatural animal. *Family Status:* s. of Loki and Svadilfari. *Career:* born from Loki while in disguise as a mare; Loki gave him to Odin as peace offering; carried Odin on many adventures. *Personality:* brave; loyal. *Distinguishing Features:* he is a white, eight-legged horse. *Supernatural Attributes:* can gallop with equal ease over land, sea or air. **Page 76, 87, 92.**

SOUTH. *Category:* Dwarf. *Career:* holding up the sky with Dwarfs, North, West and East. **Page 75.**

SUN. *Category:* human. *Family Status:* d. of Mundulfari; one d. yet to be born. *Career:* named after the planet by her father as she was so beautiful; the gods found this presumptuous and carried her away as punishment; made her drive chariot of the sun; pursued by giant wolf Skoll who is trying to catch her; Skoll will succeed when Raganarok comes but her daughter will survive and light the new world. **Page 75.**

SURT (sert) "Black". *Category:* supernatural being. *Career:* guarding gates of Muspell and ruling fiery beings who live there; at Ragnarok he will lead his hordes out of Muspell against the gods; he will set the Nine Worlds ablaze and destroy them. *Personality:* extremely fierce; terrifying. *Distinguishing Features:* he is a man-like being, blackened by fire. *Supernatural Attributes:* wields a flaming sword. **Page Page 73, 103.**

SUTTUNG (soot-ung). *Category:* Giant. *Family Status:* brother to Gilling and Braugi; one d. Gunnlod. *Career:* went to avenge Gilling's death when he was killed by Dwarfs; took pay-off of Mead of Poetry instead; placed Mead in cavern with Gunnlod on guard; boasted about the Mead; would not give Odin (in disguise as the Giant Bolverk) a sip as Braugi had promised, in payment for work Odin did; then was furious when Odin stole the Mead. *Personality:* bragging; foolish. *Distinguishing Features:* vastness. **Page 97.**

SVADILFARI (svad-ill-far-ee). *Category:* animal. *Family Status:* belonged to a Rock Giant; mated with Loki (in disguise as a mare); one s. Sleipnir. *Career:* worked for the Rock Giant; esp. known for carrying stones from quarry to rebuild Asgard's wall; used by Loki to prevent Giant completing his contract and carrying off his rewards – Loki took form of a mare and lured him into woods; Giant could not finish work without him. *Personality:* hard-working; amorous. **Page 86, 87.**

SYR (seer) "sow". See **FREYJA**

THIALFI (thyalf-ee). *Category:* human. *Family Status:* brother to Roskva. *Career:* poor peasant; his family gave shelter to Thor and Loki, on their journey to Utgard; greed got the better of him and he broke thighbone of one of Thor's goats (Thor had killed them to provide meat) to suck the marrow, though expressly forbidden to touch them; he and Roskva taken as servants by Thor in recompense; took part in race with Giant in Utgard, but lost. *Personality:* incautious. **Page 94.**

THIAZI (thyah-zee). *Category:* Giant. *Family Status:* one d. Skadi. *Career:* anti-god activity; tormented Odin, Honir and Loki on a trip to Earth by taking disguise as eagle and using magic to prevent their meat cooking; attacked by Loki so carried him off and made him promise to bring Idunn and her golden apples in return for releasing him; Loki kept bargain and Thiazi imprisoned Idunn; gods grew old and frail without apples of youth; Loki rescued Idunn; Thiazi flew after him in eagle form; met his death when he followed Loki into Asgard and was set upon by the gods; his eyes put in the sky as stars by Odin to appease Skadi when she came for revenge. *Personality:* sly; aggressive; over-confident. *Distinguishing Features:* v. big. *Supernatural Attributes:* shape-changing. **Page 89.**

THOR (thaw). *Category:* Aesir god. *Family Status:* s. of Odin and Jorth; m. Sif; many lo. incl. Jarnsaxa (two s. Modi, Magni); Giantess (one d. Thrud). *Career:* thunder-god; god of law and order; great warrior; Defender of Asgard; v. popular; loved fighting, feasting and drinking; many adventures – greatest enemy of the Giants, though they taught him a lesson when he visited Utgard; controlled storms on Earth; sometimes a figure of fun to other gods for his simplicity. *Personality:* trusting; good-natured, despite quick temper; not too brainy; v. confident of his superior strength. *Distinguishing Features:* wild red hair and beard; always in battle-dress; drove chariot pulled by giant goats. *Supernatural Attributes:* the hammer, Mjollnir; belt that doubled his strength; iron gauntlets for grasping any weapon. **Page 66, 76, 78-79, 81, 90, 91, 92, 93, 94, 95, 102, 103.**

THRALL (thrawl). *Category:* human. *Family Status:* s. of Ai and Edda, given to them by Heimdall; many children. *Career:* poor labourer; destined to be ancestor of all landless labourers. *Personality:* dull; simple. **Page 83.**

THRYM (thrim). *Category:* Giant. *Career:* famed for daring to steal Mjollnir and demand Freyja as his wife as reward for returning it; short-lived glory, though, as Thor and Loki went to Thrym's hall disguised as Freyja (in bridal veil) and bridesmaid; when Mjollnir was produced to bless the bride, Thor grabbed it and killed Thrym and many others. *Personality:* arrogant; daring; unwise. *Distinguishing Features:* huge body. **Page 93.**

TOOTHGNASHER and **TOOTHGRINDER.** *Category:* supernatural animals. *Family Status:* belonged to Thor. *Career:* pulling Thor's chariot across the sky; causing thunder on Earth with their hooves. *Distinguishing Features:* they are enormous, fearsome goats. *Supernatural Attributes:* can be eaten and revived next day by Thor. **Page 79.**

TROLLS. *Category:* supernatural beings. *Career:* enemies to the gods, esp. Thor; fighting wars. *Personality:* bad-tempered; war-like. *Distinguishing Features:* similar to Giants; huge. *Supernatural Attributes:* great strength. **Page 71, 102.**

TYR (tier). *Category:* Aesir god. *Family Status:* s. of Odin. *Career:* god of law and order; guaranteed contracts and agreements; patron of the Thing; called bravest of the gods; most admired for daring to put his hand in Fenrir's mouth when gods were trying to bind the wolf and he demanded sign of good faith that he was not being tricked; it was a trick, of course, and Fenrir bit off Tyr's hand – often called the One-Handed after this. *Personality:* honourable; great integrity; enormous courage. *Distinguishing Features:* one missing hand. **Page 80, 89, 95, 103.**

UTGARD-LOKI: (oot-guard-low-kee). *Category:* Giant. *Career:* King of the Giants; dedicated to fighting gods; notorious for getting the better of Thor when he visited Utgard; took disguise as Skrymir. *Personality:* wily; intelligent. *Distinguishing Features:* gigantic. *Supernatural Attributes:* shape-changing. **Page 94.**

VALI (vah-lee). i. See **NARVI.**

VALI (vah-lee).ii. *Category:* god. *Family Status:* s. of Odin and Giantess, Rind. *Career:* noted for killing Hod **Page 102.**

VALKYRIES (val-kye-reez) "Choosers of the Slain". *Category:* supernatural beings. *Career:* female warrior servants to Odin; directed the course of battles; chose the most valiant warriors to go to Valhalla to be Odin's guests when they were slain; also served food and drink to warriors in Valhalla. *Personality:* fearless; frightening. *Distinguishing Features:* battle-dress when choosing the slain. **Page 76, 93, 100.**

VANIR (vah-near). *Category:* gods. *Family Status:* all children of Odin.

Career: fertility gods; at first antagonistic to Aesir gods, but after war between the two types they co-operated and lived in peace; main leaders – Njord, Freyja, Freyr, Aegir, Ran, Heimdall. *Supernatural Attributes:* magic powers; witchcraft. **Page 70, 73, 82, 84, 85, 86, 87.**

VE (vay) and **VILI** (vill-ee). *Category:* gods. *Family Status:* s. of Bor and Bestla. *Career:* first gods, with Odin, their brother; helped create the Earth and first humans. **Page 74.**

VIDAR (vee-dar). *Category:* god. *Family Status:* s. of Odin and Grid. *Career:* will avenge Odin by killing Fenrir at Ragnarok; will survive and become one of the new leaders of the gods. *Personality:* noble; brave. **Page 103.**

VILI. See **VE.**

WEST. *Category:* Dwarf. *Career:* holding up the sky with Dwarfs North, South and East. **Page 75.**

YMIR (im-meer). *Category:* Giant. *Family Status:* emerged from vapours of melting snow of Niflheim; many children born from his sweat. *Career:* first Frost Giant; appeared in the emptiness known as Ginnungagap; was suckled by giant cow, Audumla; killed by Odin, Vili and Ve; his body used to form the Earth; his bones and teeth became mountains and his blood filled rivers and seas; his skull formed dome of the sky and his brains were clouds. *Personality:* brutal; evil; violent. *Distinguishing Features:* enormous; icy appearance. **Page 74-75.**

PLACES

ALFHEIM (alf-hame) "Land of the Elves". Home of the Light Elves. **Page 72, 73.**

ASGARD (ass-guard). Land of the Aesir gods. **Page 73, 80, 82, 84, 86, 88, 90, 92.**

BILSKIRNIR (bill-skier-near) "Lightning". Thor and Sif's great hall in Asgard. **Page 79.**

BREIDABLIK (brade-a-blick). Balder and Nanna's home in Asgard. **Page 80.**

GINNUNGAGAP (ghin-un-ga-gap). Great emptiness that existed between Muspell and Niflheim before the world began. **Page 74.**

HEL (hell). Land of the Dead. Ruled over by Hel. **Page 72, 81, 88.**

JOTUNHEIM (yot-oon-hame). Mountain home of the Giants. East of Midgard. **Page 72, 73, 92.**

MIDGARD (mid-guard). Home of humans; Earth. **Page 72, 73, 91, 98, 102.**

MUSPELL (moo-spell). Area of fire before Earth was created. **Page 72, 73, 74, 103.**

NIDAVELLIR (need-a vell-ear). Home of the Dwarfs. **Page 73.**

NIFLHEIM (niffle-hame). Area of ice and snow in the North before the world existed. **Page 73.**

NOATUN (noah-toon) "Shipyard". Njord's home by the sea. **Page 82.**

OCEAN. Vast stretch of water around Earth; home of Jormungand. **Page 73, 88.**

SESSRUMNIR (sess-room-near) "Many Seats". Freyja's hall in Asgard. **Page 84.**

SVARTALFHEIM (svart-alf-hame) "Land of the Dark Elves". **Page 73.**

UTGARD (oot-guard). Stronghold of the Giants; either in Jotunheim or beyond the Ocean. **Page 73, 94.**

VALASKJALF (val-ah-skyalf) "Shelf of the Slain". One of Odin's halls in Asgard. Home of throne, Hlidskjalf. **Page 76, 85.**

VALHALLA (val-hal-ah) "Hall of the Slain". One of Odin's halls in Asgard. Home of dead heroes. **Page 76.**

VANAHEIM (van-ah-hame). Land of the Vanir gods. **Page 73, 86.**

VIGARD (vee-guard). Huge plain where Ragnarok will take place. **Page 103.**

THINGS

BIFROST (bee-frost). Rainbow bridge between Asgard and Midgard. **Page 73, 82.**

BRISINGAMEN (briss-ing-a-men) "Necklace of the Brisings". Necklace made by four Dwarfs. **Page 84.**

FOUNTAIN OF MIMIR. Well in Midgard into which one of Yggdrasil's roots dips; guarded by the god Mimir; also called Fountain of Knowledge. **Page 73, 86.**

GJALL (gyall). Heimdall's horn. **Page 103.**

GUNGNIR (goong-near). Magic spear belonging to Odin. **Page 76, 90.**

HLIDSKJALF (hlid-skyalf). Odin's throne in Valaskjalf. **Page 76.**

MJOLLNIR (myoll-near). Supernatural hammer. Thor's main weapon and symbol. **Page 79, 90, 91, 92, 94, 95, 103.**

RAGNAROK (rag-na-rock). Great battle at the end of the world. Doom of the gods. **Page 102.**

SKIDBLADNIR (skid-blad-near). Magic ship made by Dwarfs. Belonged to Freyr. **Page 85, 90.**

SPRING OF HVERGELMIR (hvare-ghel-meer). Well in Niflheim into which one of Yggdrasil's roots dives; guarded by the dragon Nidhogg. **Page 73.**

WELL OF URD (oord). Well in Asgard into which one of Yggdrasil's roots plunges; tended by the Norns. **Page 73.**

YGGDRASIL (ig-dra-sill). Giant ash tree which holds the Nine Worlds in position in space. **Page 73, 87. 103.**

INDEX